Lecture Notes in Computer Science

Lecture Notes in Computer Science

Edited by G. Goos and J. Hartmanis

114

Barbara Liskov   Russell Atkinson
Toby Bloom   Eliot Moss   J. Craig Schaffert
Robert Scheifler   Alan Snyder

CLU
Reference Manual

Springer-Verlag
Berlin Heidelberg New York 1981

Author

Barbara Liskov
Toby Bloom
Robert Scheifler
J.C. Schaffert
Laboratory for Computer Science, Massachusetts Institute of Technology
545 Technology Square, Cambridge, MA 02139, USA

Russell Atkinson
Xerox Research Center
3333 Coyote Hill Road, Palo Alto, California, USA

Alan Snyder
Newlett Packard Corporation
1501 Page Mill Road, Palo Alto, California, USA

Eliot Moss
Fort Gordon, Georgia, USA

AMS Subject Classifications (1979): 68-02
CR Subject Classifications (1981): 4.2, 4.22

ISBN 3-540-10836-X Springer-Verlag Berlin Heidelberg New York
ISBN 0-387-10836-X Springer-Verlag New York Heidelberg Berlin

Printing and binding: Beltz Offsetdruck, Hemsbach/Bergstr.
2145/3140-543210

History of CLU

The development of CLU began in January 1974. By the summer of 1975, the first version of the language had been completed. Over the next two years, the entire language design was reviewed and two implementations were produced. Based on this review, and on the experience gained in using CLU, a second version of the language was designed in the fall of 1977. Since then two more implementations have been produced.

A preliminary version of this manual appeared in July 1978. Since that time, an additional statement for exception handling, an own variable mechanism, and three new built-in type generators have been added to the language, and a number of minor changes have been made to the I/O facilities. A second version of the manual appeared in October 1979. Since that time, a few operations have been added to some of the built-in types, and more minor changes have been made to the I/O facilities.

Guide to the Manual

This document serves both as an introduction to CLU and as a language reference manual. Sections 1 through 4 present an overview of the language. These sections highlight the essential features of CLU, and discuss how CLU differs from other, more conventional, languages. Sections 5 through 13 form the reference manual proper. These sections describe each aspect of CLU in detail, and discuss the proper use of various features. Appendices I through III provide concise summaries of CLU's syntax, data types, and I/O facilities. Appendix IV contains example programs.

Those readers wanting an introduction to CLU should read Sections 1 through 13 in order, concentrating on Sections 1 through 4, 8, 9, and 13. Appendix IV should also be of interest. After becoming familiar with CLU, specific questions can be answered by consulting Sections 5 through 13 and Appendices I through III.

We would greatly appreciate receiving comments on both the language and this manual. Comments should be sent to Barbara Liskov, Laboratory for Computer Science, Massachusetts Institute of Technology, 545 Technology Square, Cambridge, MA 02139.

This work was supported in part by the Advanced Research Projects Agency of the Department of Defense, monitored by the Office of Naval Research under contract N00014-75-C-0661, and in part by the National Science Foundation under grant MCS74-21892 A01.

CONTENTS

Overview

Detailed Description

Appendices

1. Modules

A CLU program consists of a group of modules. Three kinds of modules are provided, one for each kind of abstraction that we have found to be useful in program construction. Procedures support procedural abstraction, iterators support control abstraction, and clusters support data abstraction.

1.1 Procedures

A *procedure* performs an action on zero or more *argument* objects, and terminates returning zero or more *result* objects. All communication between a procedure and its invoker generally takes place through these arguments and results; a procedure has no global variables unless it is defined in a cluster that has own variables. A procedure may retain objects from one invocation to the next through the use of local own variables.

A procedure may terminate in one of a number of *conditions*. One of these is the normal condition; the others are exceptional conditions. Differing numbers and types of results may be returned in different conditions. All information about the names of conditions and the number and types of arguments and results is described in the *procedure heading*. For example,

square_root = **proc** (x: **real**) **returns (real) signals** (no_real_result)

is the heading of a square_root procedure, which takes a single real argument. Square_root terminates either in the normal condition (returning the square root of *x*) or in the no_real_result condition (returning no results).

1.2 Iterators

An *iterator* computes a sequence of *items* based on its arguments. These items are provided to its invoker one at a time. Each item consists of zero or more objects.

An iterator is invoked by a **for** statement. The iterator provides each item by *yielding* it. The objects in the item are assigned to the loop variables of the **for** statement, and the body of the **for** statement is executed. Then control is returned to the iterator so it can yield the next item in the sequence. The **for** loop is terminated when the iterator terminates, or the **for** loop body may explicitly terminate itself and the iterator.

Just like a procedure, an iterator has no global variables unless it is defined in a cluster that has own variables. An iterator may retain objects from one invocation to the next through the use of local own variables. An iterator may also terminate in one of a number of conditions. In the normal condition, no results can be returned, but different numbers and types of results can be returned in the exceptional conditions. All information about the names of conditions, and the number and types of arguments and results is described in the *iterator heading*. For example,

    leaves = **iter** (t: tree) **yields** (node)

is the heading for an iterator that produces all leaf nodes of a tree object. This iterator might be used in a **for** statement as follows:

    for leaf: node **in** leaves(x) **do**
        ... examine(leaf) ...
    end

1.3 Clusters

A *cluster* implements a data abstraction, which is a set of objects and a set of *primitive operations* to create and manipulate those objects. The operations can be either procedural or control abstractions. The *cluster heading* states what operations are available, e.g.,

    int_set = **cluster is** create, insert, elements

states that the operations of int_set are *create*, *insert*, and *elements*.

A cluster is used to implement a distinct *data type*, different from all others. Users of this type are constrained to treat objects of the type abstractly. That is, the objects may be manipulated only via the primitive operations. This means that information about how the objects are actually represented in storage may not be used.

Inside the cluster, a *concrete representation* (in terms of some other type) is chosen for the objects, and the operations are implemented in terms of this representation. Each operation is implemented by a *routine* (a procedure or iterator); these routines are exactly like those not contained in clusters, except that they can treat the objects being defined by the cluster both abstractly and in terms of the concrete representation. (The ability to treat objects abstractly is useful when defining recursive data structures, where the concrete representation makes use of the new type.) A cluster may contain additional procedures and iterators, which are purely for local use; these routines do not define operations of the type. The routines in a cluster are not considered to be separate modules; they are simply part of the cluster module.

A cluster may also contain own variables, whose lifetimes are independent of routine activations. These variables are globally available to all routines in the cluster, but are not available from outside the cluster.

1.4 Parameterized Modules

Procedures, iterators, and clusters can all be *parameterized*. Parameterization provides the ability to define a class of related abstractions by means of a single module. Parameters are limited to the following types: **int**, **real**, **bool**, **char**, **string**, **null**, and **type**. The most interesting and useful of these are the type parameters.

When a module is parameterized by a type parameter, this implies that the module was written without knowledge of what the actual parameter type would be. Nevertheless, if the module is to do anything with objects of the parameter type, certain operations must be provided by any actual type. Information about required operations is described in a **where** clause, which is part of the heading of a parameterized module. For example,

> set = **cluster** [t: **type**] **is** create, insert, elements
>   **where** t **has** equal: **proctype** (t, t) **returns (bool)**

is the heading of a parameterized cluster defining a generalized set abstraction. Sets of many different element types can be obtained from this cluster, but the **where** clause states that the element type is constrained to provide an *equal* operation.

To use a parameterized module, actual values for the parameters must be provided, using the general form

> module_name [parameter_values]

Parameter values must be computable at the time they are compiled. Providing actual parameters selects one abstraction out of the class of related abstractions defined by the parameterized module; since the values are known at compile-time, the compiler can do the selection and can check that the **where** clause restrictions are satisfied. The result of the selection, in the case of a parameterized cluster, is a type, which can then be used in declarations; in the case of parameterized procedures or iterators, a procedure or iterator is obtained, which is then available for invocation. For example, set[**int**] is a use of the set abstraction shown above, and is legal because **int** does have an *equal* operation.

A parameterized cluster, procedure, or iterator is said to implement a *type generator*, *procedure generator*, or *iterator generator*, respectively.

1.5 Program Structure

As was mentioned before, a program consists of a group of modules. Each module defines either a single abstraction or, if parameterized, a class of related abstractions. Modules are never embedded in other modules. Rather, the program is a single level structure, with all modules potentially usable by all other modules in the program.

Type-checking of inter-module references is carried out using information in the module headings, augmented, in the case of clusters, by the headings of the procedures and iterators that implement the operations.

Each module is a separate textual unit, and is compiled independently of other modules. Compilation and program construction are discussed in Section 4.

2. Data Types

One of the primary goals of CLU was to provide, through clusters, a type extension mechanism that permits user-defined types to be treated as similarly as possible to built-in types. This goal has been achieved to a large extent. Both built-in and user-defined types are viewed as providing sets of primitive operations, with access to the real representation information limited to just these operations. The ways in which built-in types differ from user-defined types will be discussed in Section 2.3 below.

2.1 Built-in Types

CLU provides a rich set of built-in types and type generators. The built-in types are **int**, **real**, **bool**, **char**, **string**, **null**, and **any**. **Int** and **real** provide the usual arithmetic and relational operations on integers and real numbers, and **bool** provides the standard boolean operations. **Char** is the full ASCII character set; the usual relational operators are provided, along with conversion to and from integers. **Strings** are (possibly empty) sequences of characters; usual string operations like selecting the *ith* character, and concatenation are provided. However, strings are somewhat unusual in that string objects cannot be modified. For example, it is not possible to change a character in a string; instead, a new string, differing from the original in that position, may be created.

Null is a type containing one object, **nil**. **Null** is used primarily in conjunction with the tagged union type discussed below.

Any is provided to permit an escape from compile-time type-checking. The type **any** introduces no new objects, but instead may be used as the type of a variable when the programmer wishes to assign objects of different types to that variable, or does not know what kind of object will be assigned to the variable. CLU provides a built-in procedure generator, **force**, which permits a run-time examination of the type of object named by a variable of type **any**.

The built-in type generators are: **array**, **sequence**, **record**, **struct**, **oneof**, **variant**, **proctype**, and **itertype**. Arrays are one-dimensional. The type of element contained in the array is specified by a type parameter, e.g., **array[int]** and **array[array[int]]**. (The latter example shows how a two-dimensional array might be handled.) CLU arrays are unusual in that they can grow dynamically. An array is often empty when first created, but there is also a special *array constructor* for specifying initial elements. Array operations can grow and shrink the array at either end, query the current size and low and high bounds of the array, and access and replace elements within the current bounds.

Sequences are immutable arrays, in that the size of a sequence can not be changed dynamically, and new elements cannot be stored into a sequence. New sequences can be constructed from existing sequences in much the same way as new strings are created. Sequence operations are culled from both string and array operations, and there is a special *sequence constructor*, which is syntactically similar to the array constructor form.

CLU records are heterogeneous collections of component objects; each component is accessed by a selector name. Records must be explicitly constructed by means of a special *record constructor*. The constructor requires that an object be provided for each component of the record; this requirement ensures that no component of the record is undefined in the sense of naming no object. Record operations permit selection of component objects and replacement of components with new objects.

Structures are immutable records, in that the components of a structure cannot be replaced with new objects. Structures are constructed by means of a *structure constructor*, which is syntactically identical to the record constructor form.

A oneof type is a tagged, discriminated union. The objects of a oneof type each consist of a *tag* (an identifier) and a component object; oneof objects with different tags may have component objects of different types. A oneof object, once created, cannot be changed. Thus, oneof types provide a capability similar to that provided by variant records in Pascal. Operations are provided for creating oneof objects. Oneof objects are usually decomposed through the **tagcase** statement.

Variants are mutable oneofs. The tag and component object of a variant can be replaced simultaneously with new values. Like oneofs, variants are usually decomposed through the **tagcase** statement.

Procedure and iterator types provide procedures and iterators as first-class objects; i.e., routines (including those in clusters) can be assigned to variables and can occur as components of other objects. These types are parameterized by all the information appearing in a procedure or iterator heading, with the exception of the formal argument names.

In addition to all the built-in types and type generators mentioned above, CLU programs may also make use of the type **type**. The use of **type** values is limited to parameters of parameterized modules; there are no arguments or variables of type **type**.

Finally, CLU provides a number of types and procedures to support I/O. The types are not considered to be built-in types of CLU, but they must be available in the library. I/O support is described in Appendix III.

2.2 User-Defined Types

Users may define new types by providing clusters that implement them. The cluster may implement a single type, or, in the case of a parameterized cluster, a group of related types. The type or types defined by a cluster are distinct from all built-in types and from all types defined by other clusters.

2.3 Comparison of User-Defined and Built-In Types

Little distinction is made between user-defined types and built-in types. Either can be used freely to declare the arguments, variables, and results of routines. In addition, in either case there is a set of primitive operations associated with the type, and the same syntax is used to invoke these operations. The ordinary syntax to name an operation is

type $ op_name

Since different types will often have operations of the same name (e.g., *create*), this compound form is used to avoid ambiguity.

For many operations there is also a customary abbreviated form of invocation, which can be used for user-defined types as well as for built-in types. There is a standard translation from each abbreviated form to the ordinary form of invocation. For example, an addition operation is usually invoked using the infix notation "x + y"; this is translated into "T$add(x, y)", where T is the type of x. Extending notation to user-defined types in this way is sometimes called *operator overloading*. We permit almost all special syntax to be overloaded; there are always constraints on the overloading definition (e.g., *add* must have two arguments and one result), but they are quite minimal.

Nevertheless, there are three main distinctions between built-in types and user-defined types:

1. Built-in type and type generator names cannot be redefined. (This is why we always show them in boldface in this document.)

2. Some built-in types, e.g., **int**, **real**, etc., have literals. There is no mechanism for defining literals for user-defined types.

3. Some built-in types are related to certain other constructs of CLU. For example, the **tagcase** statement is a control construct especially provided to permit discrimination on oneof and variant objects. In addition, in places where compile-time constants are required, e.g., as actual parameters to parameterized modules, the expressions that may appear are limited to a subset of the built-in types and their operations. One reason for this limitation is that the permitted types are known to contain only *immutable* objects (see Section 3.1).

3. Semantics

All languages present their users with some model of computation. This section describes those aspects of CLU semantics that differ from the common ALGOL-like model. In particular, we discuss the notions of objects and variables, and the definitions of assignment and argument passing that follow from these notions. We also discuss type-correctness.

3.1 Objects and Variables

The basic elements of CLU semantics are *objects* and *variables*. Objects are the data entities that are created and manipulated by programs. Variables are just the names used in a program to refer to objects.

Each object has a *type*, which characterizes its behavior. A type defines a set of primitive operations to create and manipulate objects of that type. An object may be created and manipulated only via the operations of its type.

An object may *refer* to objects. For example, a record object refers to the objects that are the components of the record. This notion is one of logical, not physical, containment. In particular, it is possible for two distinct record objects to refer to (or *share*) the same component object. In the case of a cyclic data structure, it is even possible for an object to "contain" itself. Thus, it is possible to have recursive data structure definitions and shared data objects without explicit reference types.

Objects exist independently of procedure and iterator activations. Space for objects is allocated from a dynamic storage area as the result of invoking constructor operations of certain primitive CLU types, such as records and arrays. In theory, all objects continue to exist forever. In practice, the space used by an object may be reclaimed (via garbage collection) when that object is no longer accessible. (An object is accessible if it is denoted by a variable of an active routine or an own variable of any cluster or routine, or is a component of an accessible object.)

Objects may be divided into two categories. Some objects exhibit time-varying behavior. Such an object, called a *mutable* object, has a *state* that may be modified by certain operations without changing the identity of the object. Records and arrays are examples of mutable objects. For example, replacing the *ith* element of any array *a* causes the state of *a* to change (to contain a different object as the *ith* element).

If a mutable object *m* is shared by two other objects *x* and *y*, then a modification to *m* made via *x* will be visible when *m* is examined via *y*. Communication through shared mutable objects is most beneficial in the context of procedure invocation, described below.

Objects that do not exhibit time-varying behavior are called *immutable* objects. Examples of immutable objects are integers, booleans, characters, and strings. The properties of an immutable object do not change with time. These properties generally do not include the properties of any component objects. For example, a sequence is immutable even though its elements may be mutable.

Variables are names used in programs to *denote* particular objects at execution time. Unlike variables in many common programming languages, which are containers for values, CLU variables are simply names that the programmer uses to refer to objects. As such, it is possible for two variables to denote (or *share*) the same object. CLU variables are much like those in LISP, and are similar to pointer variables in other languages. However, CLU variables are *not* objects; they cannot be denoted by other variables or referred to by objects. Thus, variables declared within one routine cannot be accessed or modified by any other routine.

3.2 Assignment and Invocation

The basic actions in CLU are *assignment* and *invocation*. The assignment primitive $x := E$, where x is a variable and E is an expression, causes x to denote the object resulting from the evaluation of E. For example, if E is a simple variable y, then the assignment $x := y$ causes x to denote the object denoted by y. The object is *not* copied; after the assignment is performed, the object will be *shared* by x and y. Assignment does not affect the state of any object.

Figure 1 illustrates these notions of object, variable, and assignment. Here we show variables in a stack, and objects in a heap (free storage area), an obvious way to implement CLU. Figure 1a contains three objects: α, β, and γ. α is an integer (in fact, 3) and is denoted by variable x, while β and γ are of type set[**int**] and are denoted by variables y and z, respectively. Figure 1b shows the result of executing

   $y := z$

Now y and z both refer to, or share, the same object, γ; β is no longer accessible, and so can be garbage collected.

Invocation involves passing argument objects from the caller to the called routine and returning result objects from the routine to the caller. The objects returned by the procedure, or yielded by an iterator, may be assigned to variables in the caller. Argument passing is defined in terms of assignment; the formal arguments of a routine are considered to be local variables of the routine and are initialized, by assignment, to the objects resulting from the evaluation of the argument expressions. We call the argument passing technique *call by sharing*, because the argument objects are shared between the caller and the called routine.

Fig. 1. Assignment

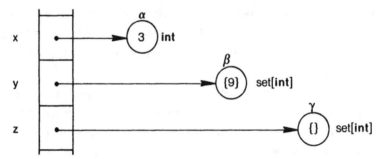

Fig 1a.

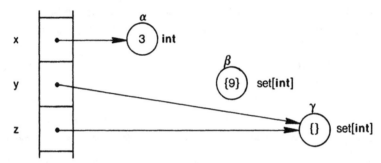

Fig 1b.

The technique does not correspond to most traditional argument passing techniques (it is similar to argument passing in LISP). In particular it is not call by value because mutations of arguments performed by the called routine will be visible to the caller. And it is not call by reference because access is not given to the variables of the caller, but merely to certain objects.

Figure 2 illustrates invocation and object mutation. Figure 2a continues from the situation shown in Figure 1b, and illustrates the situation immediately after invocation of

    set[int]$insert(y, x)

(but before executing the body of *insert*). *Insert* has two formal arguments; the first, *s*, denotes the set, and the second, *v*, denotes the integer to be inserted into *s*. Note that the variables of the caller (*x*, *y* and, *z*) are not accessible to *insert*. Figure 2b illustrates the situation after *insert* returns. Note that object γ has been modified and now refers to α (the set γ now contains 3), and since γ is shared by both *y* and *z*, the modification of γ is visible through both these variables.

Fig. 2. Invocation and object mutation

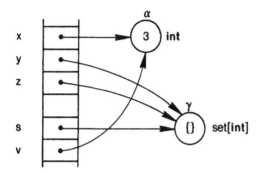

Fig 2a.

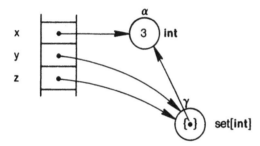

Fig 2b.

Procedure invocations may be used directly as statements; those that return exactly one object may also be used as expressions. Iterators may be invoked only through the **for** statement. Arbitrary recursion among procedures and iterators is permitted.

3.3 Type-Correctness

The declaration of a variable specifies the type of the objects which the variable may denote. In an assignment, the object denoted by the right-hand side must have the same type as the variable on the left-hand side: there are no implicit type conversions. (The type of object denoted by an expression is the return type of the outermost procedure invoked in that expression, or, if the expression is a variable or literal, the type of that variable or literal.) There is one special case; a variable declared to be of type **any** may be assigned the value of any expression.

Argument passing is defined in terms of assignment; for an invocation to be legal, it must be possible to assign the actual arguments (the objects) to the formal arguments (the variables) listed in the heading of the routine to be invoked. Furthermore, a **return** (or **yield**) statement is legal only if the result objects could be legally assigned to variables having the types stated in the routine heading.

CLU is a *type-safe* language, in that it is not possible to treat an object of type T as if it were an object of some other type S; in particular, one cannot assign an object of type T to a variable of type S (unless S is **any**). The type **any** provides an escape from compile-time type determination, and a built-in procedure generator **force** can be used to query the type of an object at run-time. However, **any** and **force** are defined in such a way that the type-safety of the language is not undermined. The type-safety of CLU, plus the restriction that only the code in a cluster may convert between the abstract type and the concrete representation, insure that the behavior of an object is indeed characterized completely by the operations of its type.

4. The Library

As was mentioned earlier, it is intended that the modules making up a program all be separate compilation units. A fundamental requirement of any CLU implementation is that it support separate compilation, with type-checking of inter-module references. This checking can be done either at compile-time or at load-time (when a group of separately compiled modules are combined together to form a program). A second fundamental requirement is that the implementation support top-down programming. The definition of CLU does not specify how an implementation should meet these requirements. However, in this section we describe a design for the current CLU implementation, which may serve as a model for others.

Our implementation is intended to make use of the CLU library, which plays a central role in supporting inter-module references. The library contains information about all abstractions. It supports incremental program development, one abstraction at a time, and, in addition, makes abstractions that are defined during the construction of one program available as a basis for subsequent program development. The information in the library permits the separate compilation of single modules, with complete type-checking at compile-time of all external references (such as procedure names).

The library provides a hierarchical name space for retrieving information about abstractions. The leaf nodes of the library are *description units* (DUs), one for each abstraction. Figure 3 illustrates the structure of the library.

A DU contains all system-maintained information about its abstraction. A sketch of the structure of a DU is shown in Figure 4. For purposes of program development and module compilation, two pieces of information must be included in the DU: implementation information, describing zero or more modules that implement the abstraction, and the interface specification. The *interface specification* is that information needed to type-check uses of the abstraction. For procedural and control abstractions, this information consists of the number and types of parameters, arguments, and results, the names of exceptional

---

Fig. 3. A sketch of the library structure showing a DU with pathname B.Y

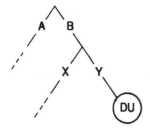

Fig. 4. A sketch showing the structure of a DU

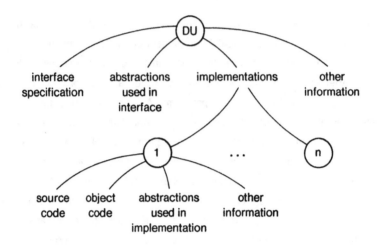

---

conditions and the number and types of results returned in each case, plus any constraints on type parameters (i.e., the **where** clause, as described in Section 1.4). For data abstractions, it includes the number and types of parameters, constraints on type parameters, and the name and interface specification of each operation.

An abstraction is entered in the library by submitting the interface specification; no implementations are required. In fact, a module can be compiled before any implementations have been provided for the abstractions that it uses; it is necessary only that interface specifications have been given for those abstractions. Ultimately, there can be many implementations of an abstraction; each implementation is required to satisfy the interface specification of the abstraction. Because all uses and implementations of an abstraction are checked against the interface specification, the actual selection of an implementation can be delayed until just before (or perhaps during) execution. We imagine a process of binding together modules into programs, prior to execution, at which time this selection would be made.

An important detail is the method by which modules refer to abstractions. To avoid the problems of name conflicts that can arise in large systems, the names used by a module to refer to abstractions can be chosen to suit the programmer's convenience. When a module is submitted for compilation, its external references must be bound to DUs so that type-checking can be performed. The binding is accomplished by constructing a *compilation environment* (CE), mapping names to DUs and constants, which is passed to the compiler along with the source code when compiling the module. A copy of the CE is stored by the compiler in the library as part of the module. A similar process is involved in entering interface specifications of abstractions, since these interfaces can include references to other (data) abstractions.

When the compiler type-checks a module, it uses the compilation environment to map the external names in the module to constants and DUs, and then uses the interface specifications in the referenced DUs to check that the abstractions are used correctly. The type-correctness of the module thus depends upon the binding of external references and the interface specifications of all referenced DUs, and could be invalidated if changes to the binding or the interface specifications were subsequently made. For this reason, the process of compilation permanently binds a module to the abstractions it uses, and the interface specification of an abstraction, once defined, is not allowed to change. Of course, a new DU can be created to describe a modified abstraction. Furthermore, during design (before any implementing modules have been entered into the system) it is reasonable to permit abstraction interfaces to change.

Typically a small to medium sized project will use only one CE, thereby establishing a consistent vocabulary for use by all programmers. Larger projects might have a number of (possibly "overlapping") CEs, each specialized for some subproject.

The library and DU structure described above can be used for purposes other than compiling and loading programs. In each case, additional information can be stored in the DU; the "other" fields shown in Figure 4 are intended to illustrate such additional information. For example, the library provides a good basis for program verification. Here the "other" information in the DU would contain a formal specification of the abstraction, and possibly some theorems that had been proved about the abstraction, while for each implementation that had been verified, an outline of the correctness proof might be retained. Additional uses of the library include retention of debugging and optimization information.

5. Notation

We use an extended BNF grammar to define the syntax. The general form of a production is:

nonterminal ::= alternative

  | alternative

  | ...

  | alternative

The following extensions are used:

a , ...   a list of one or more a's separated by commas: "a" or "a, a" or "a, a, a" etc.

{a}   a sequence of zero or more a's: " " or "a" or "a a" etc.

[a]   an optional a: " " or "a".

Nonterminal symbols appear in normal face. Reserved words appear in bold face. All other terminal symbols are non-alphabetic, and appear in normal face.

Full productions are not always shown in the body of this manual; often alternatives are presented and explained individually. Appendix I contains the complete syntax.

6. Lexical Considerations

A module is written as a sequence of tokens and separators. A *token* is a sequence of "printing" ASCII characters (octal value 40 through 176) representing a reserved word, an identifier, a literal, an operator, or a punctuation symbol. A *separator* is a "blank" character (space, vertical tab, horizontal tab, carriage return, newline, form feed) or a comment. In general, any number of separators may appear between tokens. Tokens and separators are described in more detail in the sections below.

6.1 Reserved Words

The following character sequences are reserved words:

any	down	int	record	tagcase
array	else	is	rep	then
begin	elseif	iter	resignal	true
bool	end	itertype	return	type
break	except	nil	returns	up
cand	exit	null	sequence	variant
char	false	oneof	signal	when
cluster	for	others	signals	where
continue	force	own	string	while
cor	has	proc	struct	yield
cvt	if	proctype	tag	yields
do	in	real		

Upper and lower case letters are not distinguished in reserved words. For example, 'end', 'END', and 'eNd' are all the same reserved word. Reserved words appear in bold face in this document.

6.2 Identifiers

An *identifier* is a sequence of letters, digits, and underscores that begins with a letter or underscore, and that is not a reserved word. As in reserved words, upper and lower case letters are not distinguished in identifiers.

In the syntax there are two different nonterminals for identifiers. The nonterminal *idn* is used when the identifier has scope (see Section 8.1); idns are used for variables, parameters, module names, and as abbreviations for constants. The nonterminal *name* is used when the identifier is not subject to scope rules; names are used for record and structure selectors, oneof and variant tags, operation names, and exceptional condition names.

6.3 Literals

There are literals for naming objects of the built-in types **null**, **bool**, **int**, **real**, **char**, and **string**. Their forms are discussed in Section 7.

6.4 Operators and Punctuation Symbols

The following character sequences are used as operators and punctuation symbols:

```
(        :        "        <        ~<        +        ||
)        ;        '        <=       ~<=       −        **
{        ,        \        =        ~=        *        //
}        .                 >=       ~>=       /        &
[        $                 >        ~>                 |
]        :=                                            ~
```

6.5 Comments and Other Separators

A *comment* is a sequence of characters that begins with a percent sign (%), ends with a newline character, and contains only printing ASCII characters and horizontal tabs in between. For example:

```
z := a[i] + % a comment in an expression
       b[i]
```

A *separator* is a blank character (space, vertical tab, horizontal tab, carriage return, newline, form feed) or a comment. Zero or more separators may appear between any two tokens, except that at least one separator is required between any two adjacent non-self-terminating tokens: reserved words, identifiers, integer literals, and real literals. This rule is necessary to avoid lexical ambiguities.

6.6 Semicolons

The use of semicolons (;) to terminate statements and various phrases is permitted in CLU, but semicolons are completely optional and their use is discouraged. Placement of semicolons is not shown in the body of this manual; refer to the complete syntax in Appendix I.

7. Types, Type Generators, and Type Specifications

A *type* consists of a set of objects together with a set of operations to manipulate the objects. As discussed in Section 3.1, types can be classified according to whether their objects are mutable or immutable. An immutable object (e.g, an integer) has a value that never varies, while the value (state) of a mutable object can vary over time.

A *type generator* is a *parameterized* type definition, representing a (usually infinite) set of related types. A particular type is obtained from a type generator by writing the generator name along with specific values for the parameters; for every distinct set of legal values, a distinct type is obtained. For example, the **array** type generator has a single parameter that determines the element type; **array[int]**, **array[real]**, and **array[array[int]]** are three distinct types defined by the **array** type generator. Types obtained from type generators are called *parameterized* types; others are called *simple* types.

Within a program, a type is specified by a syntactic construct called a *type_spec*. The type specification for a simple type is just the identifier (or reserved word) naming the type. For parameterized types, the type specification consists of the identifier (or reserved word) naming the type generator, together with the parameter values.

This section gives an informal introduction to the built-in types and type generators provided by CLU; many details (such as error conditions) are not discussed. Complete and precise definitions are given in Appendix II. Sections 7.1 to 7.7 describe the objects, literals, and some of the operations for each of the built-in types, while Sections 7.8 to 7.14 describe the objects, type specifications, and interesting operations of types obtained from the built-in type generators. A number of operations can be invoked using infix and prefix operators; as the various operation names are introduced, the corresponding operator, if any, will follow in parentheses.

In addition, we describe type specifications for user-defined types, and other special type specifications, in Section 7.15. The mechanism by which new types and type generators are implemented is presented in Section 13.

7.1 Null

The type **null** has exactly one immutable object, represented by the literal **nil**. The type **null** is generally used as a kind of "place filler" in a oneof or variant type (see Sections 7.12 and 7.13).

7.2 Bool

The two immutable objects of type **bool**, with literals **true** and **false**, represent logical truth values. The binary operations *equal* (=), *and* (&), and *or* (|), are provided, as well as unary *not* (~).

7.3 Int

The type **int** models (a range of) the mathematical integers. The exact range is not part of the language definition, and can vary somewhat from implementation to implementation (see Appendix II, Section 3). Integers are immutable, and are written as a sequence of one or more decimal digits. The binary operations *add* (+), *sub* (–), *mul* (∗), *div* (/), *mod* (//), *power* (∗∗), *max*, and *min* are provided, as well as unary *minus* (–) and *abs*. There are binary comparison operations *lt* (<), *le* (<=), *equal* (=), *ge* (>=), and *gt* (>). In addition, there are two operations, *from_to* and *from_to_by*, for iterating over a sequence of integers. For example, one can iterate over the odd numbers between 1 and 100 with

   for i: **int in** int$from_to_by(1, 100, 2) **do** ...*compute*... **end**

7.4 Real

The type **real** models (a subset of) the mathematical real numbers. The exact subset is not part of the language definition, although certain constraints are imposed (see Appendix II, Section 4). Reals are immutable, and are written as a *mantissa* with an optional *exponent*. A mantissa is either a sequence of one or more decimal digits, or two sequences (one of which may be empty) joined by a period. The mantissa must contain at least one digit. An exponent is 'E' or 'e', optionally followed by ' + ' or '–', followed by one or more decimal digits. An exponent is required if the mantissa does not contain a period. As is usual, $mEx = m∗10^x$. Examples of real literals are:

   3.14   3.14E0   314e–2   .0314E + 2   3.   .14

As with integers, the operations *add* (+), *sub* (–), *mul* (∗), *div* (/), *mod* (//), *power* (∗∗), *max*, *min*, *minus* (–), *abs*, *lt* (<), *le* (<=), *equal* (=), *ge* (>=), and *gt* (>), are provided. It is important to note that there is no form of *implicit* conversion between types. So, for example, the various binary operators cannot have one integer and one real argument. The *i2r* operation converts an integer to a real, *r2i* rounds a real to an integer, and *trunc* truncates a real to an integer.

7.5 Char

The type **char** provides the alphabet for text manipulation. Characters are immutable, and form an ordered set. Every implementation must provide at least 128, but no more than 512, characters; the first 128 characters are the ASCII characters in their standard order.

Printing ASCII characters (octal 40 through octal 176), other than single quote or backslash, can be written as that character enclosed in single quotes. Any character can be written by enclosing one of the following escape sequences in single quotes:

escape sequence	character
\'	' (single quote)
\"	" (double quote)
\\	\ (backslash)
\n	NL (newline)
\t	HT (horizontal tab)
\p	FF (form feed, newpage)
\b	BS (backspace)
\r	CR (carriage return)
\v	VT (vertical tab)
\•••	specified by octal value (exactly three octal digits)

The escape sequences may be written using upper case letters. Examples of character literals are:

'7'   'a'   '"'   '\"'   '\"'   '\B'   '\177'

There are two operations, *i2c* and *c2i*, for converting between integers and characters: the smallest character corresponds to zero, and the characters are numbered sequentially. Binary comparison operations exist for characters based on this numerical ordering: *lt* (<), *le* (<=), *equal* (=), *ge* (>=), and *gt* (>).

7.6 String

The type **string** is used for representing text. A string is an immutable sequence of zero or more characters. ·Strings are lexicographically ordered, based on the ordering for characters. A string is written as a sequence of zero or more character representations, enclosed in double quotes. Within a string literal, a printing ASCII character other than double quote or backslash is represented by itself. Any character can be represented by using the escape sequences listed above. Examples of string literals are:

"Item\tCost"   "altmode (\033) = \\033"   ""   " "

The characters of a string are indexed sequentially starting from one, and there are a number of operations that deal with these indexes: *fetch*, *substr*, *rest*, *indexc*, and *indexs*. The *fetch* operation is used to obtain a character by index. Invocations of *fetch* can be written using a special syntax (fully described in Section 10.7.1):

> s[i]   % get the character at index i of s

Substr returns a string given a string, a starting index, and a length:

> **string**$substr("abcde", 2, 3) = "bcd"

Rest, given a string and a starting index, returns the rest of the string:

> **string**$rest("abcde", 3) = "cde"

Indexc computes the least index at which a character occurs in a string, and *indexs* does the same for a string; the result is zero if the character or string does not occur:

> **string**$indexc('d', "abcde") = 4
> **string**$indexs("cd", "abcde") = 3
> **string**$indexs("abcde", "cd") = 0

Two strings can be concatenated together with *concat* (||), and a single character can be appended to the end of a string with *append*. Note that **string**$concat("abc", "de") and **string**$append("abcd", 'e') produce the *same* string as writing "abcde". *C2s* converts a character to a single-character string. The size of a string can be determined with *size*. *Chars* iterates over the characters of a string, from the first to the last character. There are also the usual lexicographic comparison operations: *lt* (<), *le* (<=), *equal* (=), *ge* (>=), and *gt* (>).

7.7 Any

A type specification is used to restrict the class of objects that a variable can denote, a procedure or iterator can take as arguments, a procedure can return, etc. There are times when no restrictions are desired, when any object is acceptable. At such times, the type specification **any** is used. For example, one might wish to implement a table mapping strings to arbitrary objects, with the intention that different strings could map to objects of different types. The lookup operation, used to get the object corresponding to a string, would have its result declared to be of type **any**.

The type **any** is the *union* of all possible types, and it is the *only* true union type in CLU; all other types are *base* types. Every object is of type **any**, as well as being of some base type. The type **any** has no operations; however, the base type of an object can be tested at run-time (see Section 10.13).

7.8 Array Types

Arrays are one-dimensional, and are mutable. Arrays are unconventional because the number of elements in an array can vary dynamically. Furthermore, there is no notion of an "uninitialized" element.

The *state* of an array consists of an integer called the *low bound*, and a sequence of objects called the *elements*. The elements of an array are indexed sequentially, starting from the low bound. All of the elements must be of the same type; this type is specified in the array type specification, which has the form

> **array** [type_spec]

Examples of array type specifications are

> **array[int]**
> **array[array[string]]**

There are a number of ways to create a new array, of which only two are mentioned here. The *create* operation takes an argument specifying the low bound, and creates a new array with that low bound and no elements. An array constructor can be used to create an array with an arbitrary number of initial elements. For example,

> **array[int] $ [5: 1, 2, 3, 4]**

creates an integer array with low bound 5, and four elements, while

> **array[bool] $ [true, false]**

creates a boolean array with low bound 1 (the default), and two elements. Array constructors are discussed fully in Section 10.8.1.

An array type specification states nothing about the bounds of an array. This is because arrays can grow and shrink dynamically. *Addh* adds an additional element to the end of the array, with index one greater than the previous last element. *Addl* adds an additional element to the beginning of the array, and decrements the low bound by one, so that the new first element has an index one less than the previous first element. *Remh* removes the last element; *reml* removes the first element and increments the low bound. Note that all of these operations preserve the indexes of the other elements. Also note that these operations do not create holes; they merely add to or remove from the ends of the array.

As an example, if a *remh* were performed on the integer array

> **array[int] $ [5: 1, 2, 3, 4]**

the element 4 would disappear, and the new last element would be 3, still with index 7. If a 0 were added using *addl*, it would become the new first element, with index 4.

The *fetch* operation extracts an element by index, and the *store* operation replaces an element by index; an index is illegal if no element with that index exists. Invocations of these operations can be written using special forms (covered fully in Sections 10.7.1 and 11.2.1):

```
a[i]                    % fetch the element at index i of a
a[i] := 3               % store 3 at index i of a (not really assignment)
```

The *top* and *bottom* operations return the element with the highest and lowest index, respectively. The *high* and *low* operations return the highest and lowest indexes, respectively. The *elements* iterator yields the elements from bottom to top, and the *indexes* iterator yields the indexes from low to high. There is also a *size* operation that returns the number of elements.

Every newly created array has an identity that is distinct from all other arrays; two arrays can have the same elements without being the same array object. The identity of arrays can be distinguished with the *equal* (=) operation. The *similar1* operation tests if two arrays have the same state, using the *equal* operation of the element type. *Similar* tests if two arrays have similar states, using the *similar* operation of the element type. For example, writing

    ai$[3: 1, 2, 3]

(where "ai" is equated to **array[int]**) in different places produces arrays that are similar1 and similar (but not equal), while writing the following produces arrays that are similar, but not similar1 (or equal):

    array[ai] $ [1: ai$create(1)]

7.9 Sequence Types

Sequences are immutable arrays. Although an individual sequence can have any length, that length cannot vary dynamically, and the elements of the sequence cannot be replaced. The elements of a sequence are indexed sequentially, starting from one. A sequence type specification has the form

    sequence [type_spec]

The *new* operation returns an empty sequence. A sequence constructor, which is syntactically similar to the array constructor, can be used to create a sequence with an arbitrary number of elements. Sequence constructors are discussed fully in Section 10.8.2.

Although a sequence, once created, cannot be changed, new sequences can be constructed from existing ones. *Addh* creates a new sequence with an additional element at the end (with index one greater than the last element of the old sequence). *Addl* creates a new sequence with an additional element at the beginning, with index one, so that every other element has an index one greater than its index in the old sequence. *Remh* creates a new sequence with the last element removed; *reml* creates a new sequence with the first element removed. Note that, for each of these operations, element objects are shared between the old and new sequences.

The *fetch* operation extracts an element by index, and the *replace* operation creates a new sequence with a new element at a given index; an index is illegal if no element with that index exists. Invocations of the *fetch* operation can be written using a special form (covered fully in Section 10.7.1):

> q[i]   % fetch the element at index i of q

The *top* and *bottom* operations return the element with the highest and lowest index, respectively. The *size* operation returns the number of elements. The *elements* iterator yields the elements from bottom to top, and the *indexes* iterator yields the indexes in increasing order, starting from one. Two sequences can be concatenated together with *concat* (||) to produce a new sequence, and *subseq* extracts a subsequence of a sequence.

Two sequences with the same elements are the same sequence. The *equal* (=) operation tests if two sequences have the same elements, using the *equal* operation of the element type. *Similar* tests if two sequences have similar elements, using the *similar* operation of the element type. For example, writing

> **sequence[array[int]]$[array[int]$[1]]**

in different places produces sequences that are similar but not equal.

7.10 Record Types

A record is a mutable collection of one or more named objects. The names are called *selectors*, and the objects are called *components*. Different components may have different types. A record type specification has the form

> **record** [field_spec , ...]

where

> field_spec ::= name , ... : type_spec

Selectors must be unique within a specification, but the ordering and grouping of selectors is unimportant. For example, all the of the following name the same type:

record[last, first, middle: **string**,   age: **int**]
record[first, middle, last: **string**,   age: **int**]
record[last: **string**,   age: **int**,   first, middle: **string**]

A record is created using a record constructor. For example:

info $ {last: "Jones",   first: "John",   age: 32,   middle: "J."}

(assuming that "info" has been equated to one of the above type specifications; see Section 8.3). An expression must be given for each selector, but the order and grouping of selectors need not resemble the corresponding type specification. Record constructors are discussed fully in Section 10.8.3.

For each selector "sel", there is an operation *get_sel* to extract the named component, and an operation *set_sel* to replace the named component with some other object. For example, there are *get_middle* and *set_middle* operations for the type specified above. Invocations of these operations can be written using a special form (discussed fully in Sections 10.7.2 and 11.2.2):

r.middle   % get the 'middle' component of r
r.age := 33   % set the 'age' component of r to 33 (not really assignment)

As with arrays, every newly created record has an identity that is distinct from all other records; two records can have the same components without being the same record object. The identity of records can be distinguished with the *equal* (=) operation. The *similar1* operation tests if two records have the same components, using the *equal* operations of the component types. *Similar* tests if two records have similar components, using the *similar* operations of the component types.

7.11 Structure Types

A structure is an immutable record. A structure type specification has the form

struct [field_spec , ...]

where (as for records)

field_spec ::= name , ... : type_spec

A structure is created using a structure constructor, which syntactically is identical to a record constructor. Structure constructors are discussed fully in Section 10.8.4.

For each selector "sel", there is an operation *get_sel* to extract the named component, and an operation *replace_sel* to create a new structure with the named component replaced with some other object. Invocations of the *get* operations can be written using a special form (discussed fully in Section 10.7.2):

> st.seldom   % get the 'seldom' component of st

As with sequences, two structures with the same components are in fact the same object. The *equal* (=) operation tests if two structures have the same components, using the *equal* operations of the component types. *Similar* tests if two structures have similar components, using the *similar* operations of the component types.

7.12 Oneof Types

A oneof type is a *tagged, discriminated union*. A oneof is an immutable labeled object, to be thought of as "one of" a set of alternatives. The label is called the *tag*, and the object is called the *value*. A oneof type specification has the form

> **oneof** [field_spec , ...]

where (as for records)

> field_spec ::= name , ... : type_spec

Tags must be unique within a specification, but the ordering and grouping of tags is unimportant.

As an example of a oneof type, the representation type for an immutable linked list of integers, int_list, might be written

> **oneof**[empty: **null**,
>   pair: **struct**[car: **int**, cdr: int_list]]

As another example, the contents of a "number container" might be specified by

> **oneof**[empty: **null**,
>   integer: **int**,
>   real_num: **real**,
>   complex_num: complex]

For each tag "t" of a oneof type, there is a *make_t* operation which takes an object of the type associated with the tag, and returns the object (as a oneof) labeled with tag "t". For example,

> number$make_real_num(1.37)

creates a oneof object with tag "real_num" (assuming "number" has been equated to the "number container" type specification above; see Section 8.3).

The *equal* (=) operation tests if two oneofs have the same tag, and if so, tests if the two value components are the same, using the *equal* operation of the value type. *Similar* tests if two oneofs have the same tag, and if so, tests if the two value components are similar, using the *similar* operation of the value type.

To determine the tag and value of a oneof object, one normally uses the **tagcase** statement, discussed in Section 11.6.

7.13 Variant Types

A variant is a mutable oneof. A variant type specification has the form

> **variant** [field_spec , ...]

where (as for records)

> field_spec ::= name , ... : type_spec

The state of a variant is a pair consisting of a label called the *tag* and an object called the *value*. For each tag "t" of a variant type, there is a *make_t* operation which takes an object of the type associated with the tag, and returns the object (as a variant) labeled with tag "t". In addition, there is a *change_t* operation, which takes an existing variant and an object of the type associated with "t", and changes the state of the variant to be the pair consisting of the tag "t" and the given object.

Every newly created variant has an identity that is distinct from all other variants; two variants can have the same state without being the same variant object. The identity of variants can be distinguished using the *equal* (=) operation. The *similar1* operation tests if two variants have the same tag, and if so, tests if the two value components are equal, using the *equal* operation of the value type. *Similar* tests if two variants have the same tag, and if so, tests if the two value components are similar, using the *similar* operation of the value type.

To determine the tag and value of a variant object, one normally uses the **tagcase** statement, discussed in Section 11.6.

7.14 Procedure and Iterator Types

Procedures and iterators are objects created by the CLU system (see Section 3.1). The type specification for a procedure or iterator contains most of the information stated in a procedure or iterator heading; a procedure type specification has the form

> **proctype** ([type_spec , ...]) [returns] [signals]

and an iterator type specification has the form

$$\text{itertype} \left(\left[\text{type\_spec} , \dots \right] \right) \left[\text{yields} \right] \left[\text{signals} \right]$$

where

returns   ::=   **returns** (type_spec , ...)

yields   ::=   **yields** (type_spec , ...)

signals   ::=   **signals** (exception , ...)

exception ::=   name $\left[(\text{type\_spec} , \dots) \right]$

The first list of type specifications describes the number, types, and order of arguments. The **returns** or **yields** clause gives the number, types, and order of the objects to be returned or yielded. The **signals** clause lists the exceptions raised by the procedure or iterator; for each exception name, the number, types, and order of the objects to be returned is also given. All names used in a **signals** clause must be unique, and cannot be *failure*, which has a standard meaning in CLU (see Section 12.1). The ordering of exceptions is not important. For example, both of the following type specifications name the procedure type for **string$substr**:

> **proctype (string, int, int) returns (string) signals** (bounds, negative_size)
> **proctype (string, int, int) returns (string) signals** (negative_size, bounds)

String$chars has the following iterator type:

> **itertype (string) yields (char)**

Procedure and iterator types have an *equal* (=) operation. Invocation is *not* an operation, but a primitive action of CLU semantics (see Section 9.3).

7.15 Other Type Specifications

The type specification for a user-defined type has the form

> idn $\left[[\text{constant} , \dots] \right]$

where each *constant* must be computable at compile-time (see Section 8.3). The identifier must be bound to a data abstraction (see Section 4). If the referenced abstraction is parameterized, constants of the appropriate types and number must be supplied. The order of parameters always matters in user-defined types.

There are three special type specifications that are used when implementing new abstractions: **rep, cvt,** and **type**. These forms are discussed in Sections 13.3 and 13.4. Within an implementation of an abstraction, formal parameters declared with **type** can be used as type specifications.

In addition, identifiers which have been equated to type specifications can also be used as type specifications. Equates are discussed in Section 8.3.

8. Scopes, Declarations, and Equates

We now describe how to introduce and use constants and variables, and the scope of constant and variable names. Scoping units are described first, followed by a discussion of variables, and finally constants.

8.1 Scoping Units

Scoping units follow the nesting structure of statements. Generally, a scoping unit is a body and an associated "heading". The scoping units are (refer also to Appendix I):

1. From the start of a *module* to its end.
2. From a **cluster**, **proc**, or **iter** to the matching **end**.
3. From a **for**, **do**, or **begin** to the matching **end**.
4. From a **then** or **else** in an **if** statement to the end of the corresponding body.
5. From a **tag** or **others** in a **tagcase** statement to the end of the corresponding body.
6. From a **when** or **others** in an **except** statement to the end of the corresponding body.
7. From the start of a *type_set* to its end.

In the remainder of this section we discuss only cases 1 through 6; the scope in a *type_set* is discussed in Section 13.4.

The structure of scoping units is such that if one scoping unit overlaps another scoping unit (textually), then one is fully contained in the other. The contained scope is called a *nested* scope, and the containing scope is called a *surrounding* scope.

New constant and variable names may be introduced in a scoping unit. Names for constants are introduced by equates, which are syntactically restricted to appear grouped together at or near the beginning of scoping units. For example, equates may appear at the beginning of a body, but not after any statements in the body.

In contrast, declarations, which introduce new variables, are allowed wherever statements are allowed, and hence may appear throughout a scoping unit. Equates and declarations are discussed in more detail in the following two sections.

In the syntax there are two distinct nonterminals for identifiers: *idn* and *name*. Any identifier introduced by an equate or declaration is an *idn*, as is the name of the module being defined, and any operations it has. An *idn* names a specific type or object. The other kind of identifier is a *name*. A *name* is generally used to refer to a piece of something, and is always used in context; for example, *names* are used as record selectors. The scope rules apply only to *idns*.

The scope rules are very simple:

1. An *idn* may not be redefined in its scope.

2. Any *idn* that is used as an external reference in a module may not be used for any other purpose in that module.

Unlike other "block-structured" languages, CLU prohibits the redefinition of an identifier in a nested scope. An identifier used as an external reference names a module or constant; the reference is resolved using the compilation environment (see Section 4).

8.2 Variables

Objects are the fundamental "things" in the CLU universe; variables are a mechanism for denoting (i.e., naming) objects. This underlying model is discussed in detail in Section 3. A variable has two properties: its type, and the object that it currently denotes (if any). A variable is said to be *uninitialized* if it does not denote any object.

There are only three things that can be done with variables:

1. New variables can be introduced. Declarations perform this function, and are described below.

2. An object may be assigned to a variable. After an assignment the variable denotes the object assigned. Assignment is discussed in Section 9.2.

3. A variable may be used as an expression. The value of such an expression (i.e., the result of evaluating it) is the object that the variable denotes at the time the expression is evaluated. Expressions and their evaluation are described in Section 10.

8.2.1 Declarations

Declarations introduce new variables. The scope of a variable is from its declaration to the end of the smallest scoping unit containing its declaration; hence, variables must be declared before use.

There are two sorts of declarations: those with initialization, and those without. Simple declarations (those without initialization) take the form

decl ::= idn , ... : type_spec

A simple declaration introduces a list of variables, all having the type given by *type_spec*. This type determines the types of objects that can be assigned to the variable. Some examples of simple declarations are:

i: **int**	% declare i to be an integer variable
i, j, k: **char**	% declare i, j, and k to be character variables
x, y: complex	% declare x and y to be of type complex
z: **any**	% declare z to be of type any; thus, z may denote any object

The variables introduced in a simple declaration initially denote no objects, i.e., they are uninitialized. Attempts to use uninitialized variables (if not detected at compile-time) cause the run-time exception

   failure("uninitialized variable")

(Exceptions are discussed in Section 12.)

8.2.2 Declarations with Initialization

A declaration with initialization combines declarations and assignments into a single statement. A declaration with initialization is entirely equivalent to one or more simple declarations followed by an assignment statement. The two forms of declaration with initialization are:

   idn : type_spec := expression

and

   $decl_1, \ldots, decl_n$:= invocation

These are equivalent to (respectively):

   idn : type_spec
   idn := expression

and

   $decl_1 \ldots decl_n$ % declaring $idn_1 \ldots idn_m$
   $idn_1, \ldots, idn_m$:= invocation

In the second form, the order of the idns in the assignment statement is the same as in the original declaration with initialization. (The invocation must return m objects; see Section 9.2.2.)

Some examples of declarations with initialization are:

astr: **array**[**string**] := **array**[**string**]$create(1)
> % declare astr to be an array variable and initialize it to an empty array

first, last: **string**, balance: **int** := acct$query(acct_no)
> % declare first and last to be string variables, balance an integer variable,
> % and initialize them to the results of a bank account query

The above two statements are equivalent to the following sequences of statements:

astr: **array**[**string**]
astr := **array**[**string**]$create(1)

first, last: **string**
balance: **int**
first, last, balance := acct$query(acct_no)

8.3 Equates and Constants

An equate allows a single identifier to be used as an abbreviation for a constant that may have a lengthy textual representation. An equate also permits a mnemonic identifier to be used in place of a commonly used constant, such as a numerical value. We use the term constant in a very narrow sense here: constants, in addition to being immutable, must be computable at compile-time. Constants are either types (built-in or user-defined), or objects that are the results of evaluating constant expressions. (Constant expressions are defined below.)

The syntax of equates is:

equate   ::= idn = constant
          | idn = type_set

constant ::= type_spec
          | expression

This section describes only the first form of equate; discussion of type_sets is deferred to Section 13.4.

An equated identifier may be used as an expression. The value of such an expression is the constant to which the identifier is equated. An equated identifier may not be used on the left-hand side of an assignment statement.

The scope of an equated identifier is the smallest scoping unit surrounding the equate defining it; here we mean the entire scoping unit, not just the portion after the equate. All the equates in a scoping unit must appear grouped near the beginning of the scoping unit. The exact placement of equates depends on the containing syntactic construct; usually equates appear at the beginnings of bodies.

Equates may be in any order within the group. Forward references among equates in the same scoping unit are allowed, but cyclic dependencies are illegal. For example,

```
x = y
y = z
z = 3
```

is a legal sequence of equates, but

```
x = y
y = z
z = x
```

is not. Since equates introduce idns, the scoping restrictions on idns apply (i.e., the idns may not be defined more than once).

8.3.1 Abbreviations for Types

Identifiers may be equated to type specifications, thus giving abbreviations for type names. For example:

```
at = array[int]
ot = oneof[there: rt,  none: null]
rt = record[a: foo,  b: bar]
pt = proctype (int, int) returns (int) signals (overflow)
it = itertype (int, int, int) yields (int) signals (bounds)
istack = stack[int]
mt = mark_table
```

Notice that, since equates may not have cyclic dependencies, directly recursive type specifications cannot be written. However, this does not prevent the definition of recursive types: clusters allow them to be written (see Section 13).

8.3.2 Constant Expressions

We define the subset of objects that equated identifiers may denote by stating which expressions are constant expressions. (Expressions are discussed in detail in Section 10.) A *constant expression* is an expression that can be evaluated at compile-time to produce an immutable object of a built-in type. Specifically this includes:

1. Literals.
2. Identifiers equated to constants.
3. Formal parameters (see Section 13.4).

4. Procedure and iterator names (see Section 10.5), including **force[*t*]** for any type *t*.

5. Invocations of procedure operations of the built-in constant types, provided that all operands and all results are constant expressions. However, we explicitly forbid the use of formal parameters as operands to invocations in constant expressions, since the values of formal parameters are not known at compile-time.

The built-in constant types are: **null**, **int**, **real**, **bool**, **char**, **string**, sequence types, oneof types, structure types, procedure types, and iterator types.

Some examples of equates involving expressions are:

```
hash_modulus = 29
pi = 3.14159265
win = true
control_c = '\003'
prompt_string = "Input: "
nl = string$c2s('\n')
prompt = nl || prompt_string
prompt_len = string$size(prompt)
quarter = pi / 2.0
ftb = int$from_to_by
ot = oneof[cell: cell,  none: null]
cell = record[first, second: int]
nilptr = ot$make_none(nil)
```

Note that the following equate is illegal because it uses a record constructor, which is not a constant expression:

```
cell_1_2 = ot$make_cell(cell${first: 1,  second: 2})
```

Any invocation in a constant expression must terminate normally; a program is illegal if evaluation of any constant expression would signal an exception. (Exceptions are discussed in Section 12.) Illegal programs will not be executed.

9. Assignment and Invocation

Two fundamental actions of CLU are assignment of computed objects to variables, and invocation of procedures (and iterators) to compute objects. Other actions are composed from these two by using various control flow mechanisms. Since the correctness of assignments and invocations depends on a type-checking rule, we describe that rule first, then assignment, and finally invocation.

9.1 Type Inclusion

CLU is designed to allow complete compile-time type-checking. The type of each variable is known by the compiler. Furthermore, the type of objects that could result from the evaluation of any expression (invocation) is known at compile-time. Hence, every assignment can be checked at compile-time to make sure that the variable is only assigned objects of its declared type. The rule is that an assignment $v := E$ is legal only if the set of objects defined by the type of E (loosely, the set of all objects that could possibly result from evaluating the expression) is included in the set of all objects that could be denoted by v.

Instead of speaking of the set of objects defined by a type, we generally speak of the type and say that the type of the expression must be *included in* the type of the variable. If it were not for the type **any**, the inclusion rule would be an equality rule. This leads to a simple interpretation of the type inclusion rule:

> The type of a variable being assigned an expression must be either the type of the expression, or **any**.

9.2 Assignment

Assignment is the means of causing a variable to denote an object. Some assignments are implicit, i.e., performed as part of the execution of various mechanisms of the language (most notably procedure invocation, iterator invocation, exception handling, and the **tagcase** statement). All assignments, whether implicit or explicit, are subject to the type inclusion rule. The remainder of this section discusses explicit assignments.

The assignment symbol ":=" is used in two other syntactic forms that are not true assignments, but rather abbreviations for certain invocations. These forms are used for updating collections such as records and arrays (see Section 11.2).

9.2.1 Simple Assignment

The simplest form of assignment is:

idn := expression

In this case the expression is evaluated, and the resulting object is assigned to the variable. The expression must return a single object (whose type must be included in that of the variable). Examples of simple assignments are:

```
x := 1                        % x's type must include int, i.e., it must be int or any
y := string$substr(s, 5, n)   % y's type must include string
a := array[int]$new()         % a's type must include array[int]
p := array[int]$create(3)     % p's type must include array[int]
z := (foo = bar)              % z's type must include bool
```

It is also possible to declare a variable and assign to it in a single statement; this is called a declaration with initialization, and was discussed in Section 8.2.2.

9.2.2 Multiple Assignment

There are two forms of assignment that assign to more than one variable at once:

idn , ... := expression , ...

and

idn , ... := invocation

The first form of multiple assignment is a generalization of simple assignment. The first variable is assigned the first expression, the second variable the second expression, and so on. The expressions are all evaluated (from left to right) before any assignments are performed. The number of variables in the list must equal the number of expressions, no variable may occur more than once, and the type of each variable must include the type of the corresponding expression.

This form of multiple assignment allows easy permutation of the objects denoted by several variables:

```
x, y := y, x
i, j, k := j, k, i
```

and similar simultaneous assignments of variables that would otherwise require temporary variables:

a, b := (a + b), (a – b)
quotient, remainder := (u / v), (u // v)

There is no form of this statement with declarations.

The second form of multiple assignment allows one to retain the objects resulting from an invocation returning two or more objects. The first variable is assigned the first object, the second variable the second object, and so on. The order of the objects is the same as in the **return** statement of the invoked routine. The number of variables must equal the number of objects returned, no variable may occur more than once, and the type of each variable must include the corresponding return type of the invoked procedure. Note that the right-hand side is syntactically restricted to simple invocations (see Section 10.6); sugared invocations (see Sections 10.7, 10.9) are not allowed.

Two examples of this form of assignment are:

first, last, balance := acct$query(acct_no)
x, y, z := vector$components(v)

9.3 Invocation

Invocation is the other fundamental action of CLU. In this section we discuss procedure invocation; iterator invocation is discussed in Section 11.5.2. However, up to and including passing of arguments, the two are the same.

Invocations take the form:

primary ([expression , ...])

A *primary* is a slightly restricted form of expression, which includes variables and routine names, among other things. (See the next section.)

The sequence of activities in performing an invocation are as follows:

1. The primary is evaluated. It must evaluate to a procedure or iterator.

2. The expressions are evaluated, from left to right.

3. New variables are introduced corresponding to the formal arguments of the routine being invoked (i.e., a new environment is created for the invoked routine to execute in).

4. The objects resulting from evaluating the expressions (the actual arguments) are assigned to the corresponding new variables (the formal arguments). The first formal is assigned the first actual, the second formal the second actual, and so on. The type of each expression must be included in the type of the corresponding formal argument.

5. Control is transferred to the routine at the start of its body.

An invocation is considered legal in exactly those situations where all the (implicit) assignments involved in its execution are legal.

It is permissible for a routine to assign an object to a formal argument variable; the effect is just as if that object were assigned to any other variable. From the point of view of the invoked routine, the only difference between its formal argument variables and its other local variables is that the formals are initialized by its caller.

Procedures can terminate in two ways: they can terminate *normally*, returning zero or more objects, or they can terminate *exceptionally*, signalling an exceptional condition. When a procedure terminates normally, the result objects become available to the caller, and will (usually) be assigned to variables or passed as arguments to other routines. When a procedure terminates exceptionally, the flow of control will not go to the point of return of the invocation, but rather will go to an exception handler as described in Section 12.

Some examples of invocations are:

```
p()                          % invoking a procedure taking no arguments
array[int]$create(-1)        % invoking an operation of a type
routine_table[index](input)  % invoking a procedure fetched from an array
```

10. Expressions

An expression evaluates to an object in the CLU universe. This object is said to be the *result* or *value* of the expression. Expressions are used to name the object to which they evaluate. The simplest forms of expressions are literals, variables, parameters, and routine names. These forms directly name their result object. More complex expressions are generally built up out of nested procedure invocations. The result of such an expression is the value returned by the outermost invocation.

Like many other languages, CLU has prefix and infix operators for the common arithmetic and comparison operations, and uses the familiar syntax for array indexing and record component selection (e.g., $a[i]$ and $r.s$). However, in CLU these notations are considered to be abbreviations for procedure invocations. This allows built-in types and user-defined types to be treated as uniformly as possible, and also allows the programmer to use familiar notation when appropriate.

In addition to invocation, four other forms are used to build complex expressions out of simpler ones. These are the conditional operators **cand** and **cor** (see Section 10.8), and the type conversion operations **up** and **down** (see Section 10.10).

There is a syntactically restricted form of expression called a *primary*. A primary is any expression that does not have a prefix or infix operator, or parentheses, at the top level. In certain places, the syntax requires a primary rather than a general expression. This has been done to increase the readability of the resulting programs.

As a general rule, procedures with side-effects should not be used in expressions, and programs should not depend on the order in which expressions are evaluated. However, to avoid surprises, the subexpressions of any expression are evaluated from left to right.

The various forms of expressions are explained below.

10.1 Literals

Integer, real, character, string, boolean and null literals are expressions. The syntax for literals is given in Sections 7.1 to 7.6. The type of a literal expression is the type of the object named by the literal. For example, **true** is of type **bool**, "abc" is of type **string**, etc.

10.2 Variables

Variables are identifiers that denote objects of a given type. The type of a variable is the type given in the declaration of that variable, and determines which objects may be denoted by the variable.

10.3 Parameters

Parameters are identifiers that denote constants supplied when a parameterized module is instantiated (see Section 13.4). The type of a parameter is the type given in the declaration of that parameter. Parameters of type **type** cannot be used as expressions.

10.4 Equated Identifiers

Equated identifiers denote constants. The type of an equated identifier is the type of the constant which it denotes. Identifiers equated to types and type_sets cannot be used as expressions.

10.5 Procedure and Iterator Names

Procedures and iterators may be defined either as separate modules, or within a cluster. Those defined as separate modules are named by expressions of the form:

idn $\Big[$ [constant , ...] $\Big]$

The optional constants are the parameters of the procedure or iterator abstraction. (Constants are discussed in Section 8.3.)

When a procedure or iterator is defined as an operation of a type, that type must be part of the name of the routine. The form for naming an operation of a type is:

type_spec $ name $\Big[$ [constant , ...] $\Big]$

The type of a procedure or iterator name is just the type of the named routine. Some examples of procedure and iterator names are:

```
primes
sort[int]
int$add
array[bool]$elements
```

10.6 Procedure Invocations

Procedure invocations have the form

primary ($\Big[$ expression , ... $\Big]$)

The primary is evaluated to obtain a procedure object, and then the expressions are evaluated left-to-right to obtain the argument objects. The procedure is invoked with these arguments, and the object returned is the result of the entire expression. For more discussion see Section 9.3.

The following expressions are invocations:

```
p(x)
int$add(a, b)
within[3.2](7.1, .003e7)
```

Any procedure invocation $P(E_1, ... E_n)$ must satisfy two constraints: the type of P must be of the form

proctype $(T_1, ... T_n)$ **returns** (R) **signals** (...)

and the type of each expression E_i must be included in the corresponding type T_i. The type of the entire invocation expression is given by R.

Procedures can also be invoked as statements (see Section 11.1).

10.7 Selection Operations

Arrays, sequences, records, and structures are collections of objects. Selection operations provide access to the individual elements or components of the collection. Simple notations are provided for invoking the *fetch* and *store* operations of array types, the *fetch* operation of sequence types, the *get* and *set* operations of record types, and the *get* operations of structure types. In addition, these "syntactic sugarings" for selection operations may be used for user-defined types with the appropriate properties.

10.7.1 Element Selection

An element selection expression has the form:

primary [expression]

This form is just syntactic sugar for an invocation of a *fetch* operation, and is completely equivalent to:

T$fetch(primary, expression)

where T is the type of *primary*. For example, if *a* is an array of integers, then

a[27]

is completely equivalent to the invocation

array[int]$fetch(a, 27)

When *primary* is an **array**[S] or **sequence**[S] for some type S, *expression* must be an **int**, and the result has type S. However, the element selection expression is not restricted to arrays and sequences. The expression is legal whenever the corresponding invocation is legal. In other words, T (the type of *primary*) must provide a procedure operation named *fetch*, which takes two arguments whose types include the types of *primary* and *expression*, and which returns a single result.

The use of *fetch* for user-defined types should be restricted to types with array-like behavior. Objects of such types will contain (along with other information) a collection of objects, where the collection can be indexed in some way. For example, it might make sense for an associative_memory type to provide a *fetch* operation to access the value associated with a key. *Fetch* operations are intended for use in expressions; thus they should never have side-effects.

Array-like types may also provide a *store* operation (see Section 11.2.1).

10.7.2 Component Selection

The component selection expression has the form:

primary . name

This form is just syntactic sugar for an invocation of a *get_name* operation, and is completely equivalent to:

T$get_name(primary)

where T is the type of *primary*. For example, if *x* has type **record**[first: **int**, second: **real**], then

x.first

is completely equivalent to

record[first: **int**, second: **real**]$get_first(x)

When T is a record or structure type, then T must have a selector called *name*, and the type of the result will be the type of the component named by that selector. However, the component selection expression is not restricted to records and structures. The statement is legal whenever the corresponding invocation is legal. In other words, T (the type of *primary*) must provide a procedure operation named *get_name*, which takes one argument whose type includes the type of *primary*, and which returns a single result.

The use of *get* operations for user-defined types should be restricted to types with record-like behavior. Objects of such types will contain (along with other information) one or more named objects. For example, it might make sense for a type which implements channels to files to provide a get_author operation, which returns the name of the file's creator. *Get* operations are intended for use in expressions; thus they should never have side-effects.

Types with named components may also provide *set* operations (see Section 11.2.2).

10.8 Constructors

Constructors are expressions that enable users to create and initialize arrays, sequences, records, and structures. Constructors are not provided for user-defined types.

10.8.1 Array Constructors

An array constructor has the form:

> type_spec $ [[expression:] [expression , ...]]

The type specification must name an array type: **array**[T]. This is the type of the constructed array. The expression preceding the ":" must evaluate to an integer, and becomes the low bound of the constructed array. If this expression is omitted, the low bound is 1. The expressions following the ":" are evaluated to obtain the elements of the array. They correspond (left to right) to the indexes *low_bound*, *low_bound* + 1, *low_bound* + 2, ... For an array of type **array**[T], the type of each element expression in the constructor must be included in T.

For example, the expression

> **array**[**bool**] $ [79: **true**, **false**]

constructs a new boolean array with two elements: **true** (at index 79), and **false** (at index 80). The expression

> **array**[ai] $ [ai$[], ai$[]]

(where *ai* is equated to **array**[**int**]) creates two distinct integer arrays, both empty, and creates a third array to hold them. The low bound of each array is 1.

An array constructor is computationally equivalent to an array *create* operation, followed by a number of array *addh* operations. However, such a sequence of operations cannot be written as an expression.

10.8.2 Sequence Constructors

A sequence constructor has the form:

type_spec $ [$\Big[$ expression , ... $\Big]$]

The type specification must name a sequence type: **sequence**[T]. This is the type of the constructed sequence. The expressions are evaluated to obtain the elements of the sequence. They correspond (left to right) to the indexes 1, 2, 3, ... For a sequence of type **sequence**[T], the type of each element expression in the constructor must be included in T.

A sequence constructor is computationally equivalent to a sequence *new* operation, followed by a number of sequence *addh* operations.

10.8.3 Record Constructors

A record constructor has the form:

type_spec $ { field , ... }

where

field ::= name , ... : expression

Whenever a field has more than one name, it is equivalent to a sequence of fields, one for each name. Thus, the following two constructors are equivalent:

```
R = record[ a: int,  b: int,  c: int ]
R${a, b: 7,  c: 9}
R${a: 7,  b: 7,  c: 9}
```

In a record constructor, the type specification must name a record type: **record**[S_1:T_1, ..., S_n:T_n]. This will be the type of the constructed record. The component names in the field list must be exactly the names S_1, ..., S_n, although these names may appear in any order. The expressions are evaluated left to right, and there is one evaluation per component name even if several component names are grouped with the same expression. The type of the expression for component S_i must be included in T_i. The results of these evaluations form the components of a newly constructed record. This record is the value of the entire constructor expression.

As an example, consider the following record constructor:

```
AS = array[string]
RT = record[list1, list2: AS,   item: int]
RT${item: 2,   list1, list2: AS$["Susan", "George", "Jan"]}
```

This produces a record that contains an integer and two distinct (but similar1) arrays. The arrays are distinct because the array constructor expression is evaluated twice, once for *list1* and once for *list2*.

A record constructor is computationally equivalent to a record *create* operation (see Appendix II), but that operation is not available to the user.

10.8.4 Structure Constructors

A structure constructor has the form:

    type_spec $ { field , ... }

where (as for records)

    field ::= name , ... : expression

Whenever a field has more than one name, it is equivalent to a sequence of fields, one for each name.

In a structure constructor, the type specification must name a structure type: **struct** $[S_1:T_1, ..., S_n:T_n]$. This will be the type of the constructed structure. The component names in the field list must be exactly the names $S_1, ..., S_n$, although these names may appear in any order. The expressions are evaluated left to right, and there is one evaluation per component name even if several component names are grouped with the same expression. The type of the expression for component S_i must be included in T_i. The results of these evaluations form the components of a newly constructed structure. This structure is the value of the entire constructor expression.

A structure constructor is computationally equivalent to a structure *create* operation (see Appendix II), but that operation is not available to the user.

10.9 Prefix and Infix Operators

CLU allows prefix and infix notation to be used as a shorthand for the following operations. The table shows the shorthand form and the equivalent expanded form for each operation. For each operation, the type T is the type of the first operand.

Shorthand form	Expansion
$expr_1 ** expr_2$	$T\$power(expr_1, expr_2)$
$expr_1 // expr_2$	$T\$mod(expr_1, expr_2)$
$expr_1 / expr_2$	$T\$div(expr_1, expr_2)$
$expr_1 \cdot expr_2$	$T\$mul(expr_1, expr_2)$
$expr_1 \| \| expr_2$	$T\$concat(expr_1, expr_2)$
$expr_1 + expr_2$	$T\$add(expr_1, expr_2)$
$expr_1 - expr_2$	$T\$sub(expr_1, expr_2)$
$expr_1 < expr_2$	$T\$lt(expr_1, expr_2)$
$expr_1 <= expr_2$	$T\$le(expr_1, expr_2)$
$expr_1 = expr_2$	$T\$equal(expr_1, expr_2)$
$expr_1 >= expr_2$	$T\$ge(expr_1, expr_2)$
$expr_1 > expr_2$	$T\$gt(expr_1, expr_2)$
$expr_1 \sim< expr_2$	$\sim (expr_1 < expr_2)$
$expr_1 \sim<= expr_2$	$\sim (expr_1 <= expr_2)$
$expr_1 \sim= expr_2$	$\sim (expr_1 = expr_2)$
$expr_1 \sim>= expr_2$	$\sim (expr_1 >= expr_2)$
$expr_1 \sim> expr_2$	$\sim (expr_1 > expr_2)$
$expr_1 \& expr_2$	$T\$and(expr_1, expr_2)$
$expr_1 \| expr_2$	$T\$or(expr_1, expr_2)$
$- expr$	$T\$minus(expr)$
$\sim expr$	$T\$not(expr)$

Operator notation is used most heavily for the built-in types, but may be used for user-defined types as well. When these operations are provided for user-defined types, they should always be side-effect free, and they should mean roughly the same thing as they do for the built-in types. For example, the comparison operations should only be used for types that have a natural partial or total order. Usually, the comparison operations (*lt*, *le*, *equal*, *ge*, *gt*) will be of type

proctype (T, T) **returns (bool)**

the other binary operations (e.g., add, sub) will be of type

proctype (T, T) **returns** (T) **signals** (...)

and the unary operations will be of type

proctype (T) **returns** (T) **signals** (...)

10.10 Cand and Cor

Two additional binary operators are provided. These are the conditional *and* operator, **cand**, and the conditional *or* operator, **cor**.

expression$_1$ **cand** expression$_2$

is the boolean *and* of expression$_1$ and expression$_2$. However, if expression$_1$ is **false**, expression$_2$ is never evaluated.

expression$_1$ **cor** expression$_2$

is the boolean *or* of expression$_1$ and expression$_2$, but expression$_2$ is not evaluated unless expression$_1$ is **false**. For both **cand** and **cor**, expression$_1$ and expression$_2$ must have type **bool**.

Conditional expressions can be used to avoid run-time errors. For example, the following boolean expressions can be used without fear of "bounds" or "zero_divide" errors:

```
(low_bound <= i)  cand  (i <= high_bound)  cand  (A[i] ~= 0)
(n = 0)  cor  (1000 // n = 0)
```

Because of the conditional expression evaluation involved, uses of **cand** and **cor** are not equivalent to any procedure invocation.

10.11 Precedence

When an expression is not fully parenthesized, the proper nesting of subexpressions might be ambiguous. The following precedence rules are used to resolve such ambiguity. The precedence of each infix operator is given in the table below. Higher precedence operations are performed first. Prefix operators always have precedence over infix operators.

The precedence for infix operators is as follows:

Precedence	Operators
5	**
4	* / //
3	+ - ||
2	< <= = >= > ~< ~<= ~= ~>= ~>
1	& cand
0	| cor

The order of evaluation for operators of the same precedence is left to right, except for ••, which is right to left.

The following examples illustrate the precedence rules.

Expression	Equivalent Form
a + b // c	a + (b // c)
a + b – c	(a + b) – c
a + b •• c •• d	a + (b •• (c •• d))
a = b | c = d	(a = b) | (c = d)
– a • b	(–a) • b

10.12 Up and Down

There are no implicit type conversions in CLU. Two forms of expression exist for explicit conversions. These are:

> **up** (expression)
> **down** (expression)

Up and **down** may be used only within the body of a cluster operation. **Up** changes the type of the expression from the representation type of the cluster to the abstract type. **Down** converts the type of the expression from the abstract type to the representation type. These conversions are explained further in Section 13.3.

10.13 Force

CLU has a single built-in procedure generator called **force**. **Force** takes one type parameter, and is written

> **force** [type_spec]

The procedure **force**[T] has type

> **proctype (any) returns** (T) **signals** (wrong_type)

If **force**[T] is applied to an object that is included in type T, then it returns that object. If **force**[T] is applied to an object that is not included in type T, then it signals "wrong_type" (see Section 12).

Force is a necessary companion to the type **any**. The type **any** allows programs to pass around objects of arbitrary type. However, to do anything substantive with an object, one must use the primitive operations of that object's type. This raises a conflict with compile-time type-checking, since an operation can be applied only when the arguments are known to be of the correct types. This conflict is resolved by using **force**. **Force**[T] allows a program to check, at run-time, that a particular object is actually of type T. If this check succeeds, then the object can be used in all the ways appropriate for objects of type T.

For example, the procedure **force**[T] allows us to legally write the following code:

```
x: any := 3
y: int := force[int](x)
```

while the following is illegal:

```
x: any := 3
y: int := x
```

because the type of y (**int**) does not include the type of the expression x (**any**).

11. Statements

In this section, we describe most of the statements of CLU. We omit discussion of the **signal**, **exit**, and **except** statements, which are used for signalling and handling exceptions, as described in Section 12.

CLU is a statement-oriented language, i.e., statements are executed for their side-effects and do not return any values. Most statements are *control* statements that permit the programmer to define how control flows through the program. The real work is done by the *simple* statements: assignment and invocation. Assignment has already been discussed in Section 9; the invocation statement is discussed in Section 11.1 below. Two special statements that look like assignments but are really invocations are discussed in Section 11.2.

The syntax of CLU is defined to permit a control statement to control a group of equates, declarations, and statements rather than just a single statement. Such a group is called a *body*, and has the form

$$ \text{body} ::= \left\{ \begin{array}{l} \text{equate} \\ \text{statement} \end{array} \right\} \quad \text{\% statements include declarations}$$

Scope rules for bodies are discussed in Section 8.1. No special terminator is needed to signify the end of a body; reserved words used in the various compound statements serve to delimit the bodies. Occasionally it is necessary to explicitly indicate that a group of statements should be treated like a single statement; this is done by the block statement, discussed in Section 11.3.

The conditional statement is discussed in Section 11.4. Loop statements are discussed in Section 11.5, as are some special statements that control termination of a single iteration or a single loop. The **tagcase** statement is discussed in Section 11.6. Finally, the **return** statement is discussed in Section 11.7, and the **yield** statement in Section 11.8.

11.1 Procedure Invocation

An invocation statement invokes a procedure. Its form is the same as an invocation expression:

$$ \text{primary} \left(\left[\text{expression} , \ldots \right] \right) $$

The primary must evaluate to a procedure object, and the type of each expression must be included in the type of the corresponding formal argument for that procedure. The procedure may or may not return results; if it does return results, they are discarded.

For example, the statement

array[int]$remh(a)

will remove the top element of *a* (assuming *a* is an **array[int]**). *Remh* also returns the top element, but it is discarded in this case.

11.2 Update Statements

Two special statements are provided for updating components of records and arrays. In addition they may be used with user-defined types with the appropriate properties. These statements resemble assignments syntactically, but are really invocations.

11.2.1 Element Update

The element update statement has the form

primary [expression$_1$] := expression$_2$

This form is merely syntactic sugar for an invocation of a *store* operation, and is completely equivalent to the invocation statement

T$store(primary, expression$_1$, expression$_2$)

where T is the type of *primary*. For example, if *a* is an array of integers,

a[27] := 3

is completely equivalent to the invocation statement

array[int]$store(a, 27, 3)

The element update statement is not restricted to arrays. The statement is legal if the corresponding invocation statement is legal. In other words, T (the type of *primary*) must provide a procedure operation named *store*, which takes three arguments whose types include those of *primary*, *expression$_2$*, and *expression$_2$*, respectively. In case *primary* is an **array[S]** for some type S, *expression$_1$* must be an integer, and *expression$_2$* must be included in S.

We recommend that the use of *store* for user-defined types be restricted to types with array-like behavior, i.e., types whose objects contain mutable collections of indexable elements. For example, it might make sense for an associative_memory type to provide a *store* operation for changing the value associated with a key. Such types may also provide a *fetch* operation (see Section 10.7.1).

11.2.2 Component Update

The component update statement has the form

primary . name := expression

This form is merely syntactic sugar for an invocation of a *set_name* operation, and is completely equivalent to the invocation statement

T$set_*name*(primary, expression)

where T is the type of *primary*. For example, if *x* has type **record**[first: **int**, second: **real**], then

x.first := 6

is completely equivalent to

record[first: **int**, second: **real**]$set_first(x, 6)

The component update statement is not restricted to records. The statement is legal if the corresponding invocation statement is legal. In other words, T (the type of *primary*) must provide a procedure operation called *set_name*, which takes two arguments whose types include the types of *primary* and *expression*, respectively. When T is a record type, then T must have a selector called *name*, and the type of *expression* must be included in the type of the component named by that selector.

We recommend that *set* operations be provided for user-defined types only if record-like behavior is desired, i.e., it is meaningful to permit some parts of the abstract object to be modified by selector name. In general, *set* operations should not perform any substantial computation, except possibly checking that the arguments satisfy certain constraints. For example, in a bank account type, there might be a *set_min_balance* operation to set what the minimum balance in the account must be. However, *deposit* and *withdraw* operations make more sense than a *set_balance* operation, even though the *set_balance* operation could compute the amount deposited or withdrawn and enforce semantic constraints.

Types with named components may also provide *get* operations (see Section 10.7.2).

11.3 Block Statement

The block statement permits a sequence of statements to be grouped together into a single statement. Its form is

begin body **end**

Since the syntax already permits bodies inside control statements, the main use of the block statement is to group statements together for use with the **except** statement (see Section 12).

11.4 Conditional Statement

The form of the conditional statement is

> **if** expression **then** body
> $\left\{\ \textbf{elseif}\ \text{expression}\ \textbf{then}\ \text{body}\ \right\}$
> $\left[\ \textbf{else}\ \text{body}\ \right]$
> **end**

The expressions must be of type **bool**. They are evaluated successively until one is found to be true. The body corresponding to the first true expression is executed, and the execution of the **if** statement then terminates. If none of the expressions is true, then the body in the **else** clause is executed (if the **else** clause exists). The **elseif** form provides a convenient way to write a multi-way branch.

11.5 Loop Statements

There are two forms of loop statements: the **while** statement and the **for** statement. Also provided are a **continue** statement, to terminate the current cycle of a loop, and a **break** statement, to terminate the innermost loop. These are discussed below.

11.5.1 While Statement

The **while** statement has the form:

> **while** expression **do** body **end**

Its effect is to repeatedly execute the body as long as the expression remains true. The expression must be of type **bool**. If the value of the expression is true, the body is executed, and then the entire **while** statement is executed again. When the expression evaluates to false, execution of the **while** statement terminates.

11.5.2 For Statement

The only way an iterator (see Section 13.2) can be invoked is by use of a **for** statement. The iterator produces a sequence of *items* (where an item is a group of zero or more objects) one item at a time; the body of the **for** statement is executed for each item in the sequence.

The **for** statement has the form:

for $\left[\ \text{idn}\ ,\ ...\ \right]$ **in** invocation **do** body **end**

or

for $\left[\ \text{decl}\ ,\ ...\ \right]$ **in** invocation **do** body **end**

The invocation must be an iterator invocation. The *idn* form uses previously declared variables to serve as the loop variables, while the *decl* form introduces new variables, local to the **for** statement, for this purpose. In either case, the type of each variable must include the corresponding yield type of the invoked iterator.

Execution of the **for** statement proceeds as follows. First the iterator is invoked, and it either yields an item or terminates. If the iterator yields an item, its execution is temporarily suspended, the objects in the item are assigned to the loop variables, and the body of the **for** statement is executed. The next cycle of the loop is begun by resuming execution of the iterator from its point of suspension. Whenever the iterator terminates, the entire **for** statement terminates.

An example of a **for** statement is

```
a: array[int]
    ...
sum: int := 0
for x: int in array[int]$elements(a) do
    sum := sum + x
    end
```

which will compute the sum of all the integers in an array of integers. This example makes use of the *elements* iterator on arrays, which yields the elements of the array one by one.

11.5.3 Continue Statement

The **continue** statement has the form

continue

Its effect is to terminate execution of the body of the smallest loop statement in which it appears, and to start the next cycle of that loop (if any).

11.5.4 Break Statement

The **break** statement has the form

break

Its effect is to terminate execution of the smallest loop statement in which it appears. Execution continues with the statement following that loop.

For example,

```
sum: int := 0
for x: int in array[int]$elements(a) do
    sum := sum + x
    if sum >= 100
       then sum := 100   break   end
    end
```

computes the minimum of 100 and the sum of the integers in *a*. Note that execution of the **break** statement will terminate both the iterator and the **for** loop, continuing with the statement following the **for** loop.

11.6 Tagcase Statement

The **tagcase** statement is a special statement provided for decomposing oneof and variant objects. Recall that a oneof or variant type is a discriminated union, and each object contains a *tag* and some other object called the *value* (see Sections 7.12 and 7.13). The **tagcase** statement permits the selection of a body to perform based on the tag of the object.

The form of the **tagcase** statement is

```
tagcase expression
   tag_arm { tag_arm }
   [ others : body ]
   end
```

where

tag_arm ::= **tag** name , ... [(idn: type_spec)] : body

The expression must evaluate to a oneof or variant object. The tag of this object is then matched against the names on the tag_arms. When a match is found, if a declaration (*idn: type_spec*) exists, the value component of the object is assigned to the local variable *idn*. The matching body is then executed; *idn* is defined only in that body. If no match is found, the body in the **others** arm is executed.

In a syntactically correct **tagcase** statement, the following constraints are satisfied. The type of the expression must be some oneof or variant type, T. The tags named in the tag_arms must be a subset of the tags of T, and no tag may occur more than once. If all tags of T are present, there is no **others** arm; otherwise an **others** arm must be present. Finally, on any tag_arm containing a declaration (*idn*: *type_spec*), *type_spec* must equal (not include) the type specified as corresponding in T to the tag or tags named in the tag_arm.

An example of a **tagcase** statement is

```
pair = struct[car: int,  cdr: int_list]
x: oneof[pair: pair,  empty: null]
  ...
while true do
  tagcase x
    tag empty:  return(false)
    tag pair (p: pair):  if p.car = i
                         then return(true)
                         else x := down(p.cdr)
                         end
    end
end
```

This statement might be used in a list (of integers) operation that determines whether some given integer (*i*) is on the list.

11.7 Return Statement

The form of the **return** statement is:

$$\textbf{return} \left[\, (\, \text{expression} \, , \, \text{...} \,) \, \right]$$

The **return** statement terminates execution of the containing procedure or iterator. If the **return** statement is in a procedure, the type of each expression must be included in the corresponding return type of the procedure. The expressions (if any) are evaluated from left to right, and the objects obtained become the results of the procedure. If the **return** statement occurs in an iterator no results can be returned.

For example, inside a procedure of type

proctype (...) returns (int, char)

the statement

return(3, 'a')

is legal and returns the two result objects 3 and 'a'.

11.8 Yield Statement

Yield statements may occur only in the body of an iterator. The form of a **yield** statement is:

$$\textbf{yield} \left[\, (\, \text{expression} \, , \, \dots \,) \, \right]$$

It has the effect of suspending operation of the iterator, and returning control to the invoking **for** statement. The values obtained by evaluating the expressions (left to right) are passed to the **for** statement to be assigned to the corresponding list of identifiers. The type of each expression must be included in the corresponding yield type of the iterator. After the body of the **for** loop has been executed, execution of the iterator is resumed at the statement following the **yield** statement.

12. Exception Handling and Exits

A routine is designed to perform a certain task. However, in some cases that task may be impossible to perform. In such a case, instead of returning normally (which would imply successful performance of the intended task), the routine should notify its caller by signalling an *exception*, consisting of a descriptive name and zero or more result objects.

For example, the procedure **string$fetch** takes a string and an integer index and returns the character of the string with the given index. However, if the integer is not a legal index into the string, the exception *bounds* is signalled instead. The type specification of a routine contains a description of the exceptions it may signal; for example, **string$fetch** is of type

proctype (string, int) returns (char) signals (bounds)

The exception handling mechanism consists of two parts, the signalling of exceptions and the handling of exceptions. Signalling is the way a routine notifies its caller of an exceptional condition; handling is the way the caller responds to such notification. A signalled exception always goes to the immediate caller, and the exception must be handled in that caller. When a routine signals an exception, the current activation of that routine terminates and the corresponding invocation (in the caller) is said to *raise* the exception. When an invocation raises an exception, control immediately transfers to the closest applicable handler. Handlers are attached to statements; when execution of the handler completes, control passes to the statement following the one to which the handler is attached.

The exception *failure* serves as a general catch-all error indication. When raised, it implies that some lower-level abstraction has failed in an unexpected (and possibly catastrophic) way. *Failure* is accompanied by a string result explaining the reason for the failure. All routines can potentially signal *failure*. *Failure* is implicitly part of all routine headings and routine types; a **signals** clause must not list *failure* explicitly.

12.1 Signal Statement

An exception is signalled with a **signal** statement, which has the form:

signal name $\big[$ (expression , ...) $\big]$

A **signal** statement may appear anywhere in the body of a routine. The execution of a **signal** statement begins with evaluation of the expressions (if any), from left to right, to produce a list of *exception results*. The activation of the routine is then terminated. Execution continues in the caller as described in Section 12.2 below.

The exception name must be either one of the exception names listed in the routine heading, or *failure*. If the corresponding exception specification in the heading has the form

$$name(T_1, ..., T_n)$$

then there must be exactly *n* expressions in the **signal** statement, and the type of the *ith* expression must be included in T_i. If the name is *failure*, then there must be exactly one expression present, of type **string**.

The following useless procedure contains a number of examples of **signal** statements:

```
signaller = proc (i: int) returns (int) signals (zero, negative(int))
            if i < 0 then signal negative(-i)
             elseif i > 0 then return(i)
             elseif i = 0 then signal zero
             else signal failure("unreachable statement executed!")
             end
           end signaller
```

12.2 Except Statement

When a routine activation terminates by signalling an exception, the corresponding invocation (the text of the call) is said to *raise* that exception. By attaching handlers to statements, the caller can specify the action to be taken when an exception is raised.

A statement with handlers attached is called an **except** statement, and has the form:

$$statement\ \textbf{except} \left\{ when\_handler \right\}$$
$$\left[others\_handler \right]$$
$$\textbf{end}$$

where

when_handler   ::=   **when** name , ... $\left[(decl , ...) \right]$: body

    | **when** name , ... (*) : body

others_handler ::=   **others** $\left[(idn : type\_spec) \right]$: body

Let *S* be the statement to which the handlers are attached, and let *X* be the entire **except** statement. Each when_handler specifies one or more exception names and a body. The body is executed if an exception with one of those names is raised by an invocation in *S*. All of the names listed in the when_handlers must be distinct. The optional others_handler is used to handle all exceptions not explicitly named in the when_handlers. The statement *S* can be any form of statement, and can even be another **except** statement.

If, during the execution of S, some invocation in S raises an exception E, control immediately transfers to the closest applicable handler; i.e., the closest handler for E that is attached to a statement containing the invocation. When execution of the handler completes, control passes to the statement following the one to which the handler is attached. Thus if the closest handler is attached to S, the statement following X is executed next. If execution of S completes without raising an exception, the attached handlers are not executed.

An exception raised inside a handler is treated the same as any other exception: control passes to the closest handler for that exception. Note that an exception raised in some handler attached to S cannot be handled by any handler attached to S; either the exception is handled within the handler, or it is handled by some handler attached to a statement containing X.

We now consider the forms of handlers in more detail. The form

> **when** name , ... $\Big[$ (decl , ...) $\Big]$: body

is used to handle exceptions with the given names when the exception results are of interest. The optional declared variables, which are local to the handler, are assigned the exception results before the body is executed. Every exception potentially handled by this form must have the same number of results as there are declared variables, and the types of the results must equal (not include) the types of the variables. The form

> **when** name , ... (•) : body

handles all exceptions with the given names, regardless of whether or not there are exception results; any actual results are discarded. Hence exceptions with differing numbers and types of results can be handled together.

The form

> **others** $\Big[$ (idn : type_spec) $\Big]$: body

is optional, and must appear last in a handler list. This form handles any exception not handled by other handlers in the list. If a variable is declared, it must be of type **string**. The variable, which is local to the handler, is assigned a lower case string representing the actual exception name; any results are discarded.

Note that exception results are ignored when matching exceptions to handlers; only the names of exceptions are used. Thus the following is illegal, in that **int$div** signals zero_divide without any results, but the closest handler has a declared variable:

```
begin
y: int := 0
x: int := 3 / y
  except when zero_divide (z: int): return end
end
  except when zero_divide: return end
```

An invocation need not be surrounded by **except** statements that handle all potential exceptions. This policy was adopted because in many cases the programmer can prove that a particular exception will not arise. For example, the invocation **int$div**(x, 7) will never signal zero_divide. However, this policy does lead to the possibility that some invocation may raise an exception for which there is no handler. To avoid this situation, every routine body is contained in an implicit **except** statement of the form

```
begin routine_body end
  except when failure (s: string): signal failure(s)
          others (s: string):     signal failure("unhandled exception: " || s)
          end
```

Failure exceptions are propagated unchanged; an exception named *name* becomes

failure("unhandled exception: *name*")

12.3 Resignal Statement

A **resignal** statement is a syntactically abbreviated form of exception handling:

statement **resignal** name , ...

Each name listed must be distinct, and each must be either one of the condition names listed in the routine heading, or *failure*. The **resignal** statement acts like an **except** statement containing a handler for each condition named, where each handler simply signals that exception with exactly the same results. Thus, if the **resignal** clause names an exception with a specification in the routine heading of the form

$name(T_1, ..., T_n)$

then effectively there is a handler of the form

when name $(x_1: T_1, ..., x_n: T_n)$: **signal** name$(x_1, ..., x_n)$

As for an explicit handler of this form, every exception potentially handled by this implicit handler must have the same number of results as declared in the exception specification, and the types of the results must equal the types listed in the exception specification.

As a simple example, if a routine has a **signals** clause of the form

signals (underflow, overflow)

then

x: **real** := 3.14159 * y * y
resignal underflow, overflow

is equivalent to

x: **real** := 3.14159 * y * y
except when underflow: **signal** underflow
when overflow: **signal** overflow
end

12.4 Exit Statement

A *local* transfer of control can be effected by using an **exit** statement, which has the form:

exit name $\left[\,(\,\text{expression}\,,\,\dots\,)\,\right]$

An **exit** statement is similar to a **signal** statement except that where the **signal** statement *signals* an exception to the *calling* routine, the **exit** statement *raises* the exception directly in the *current* routine. An exception raised by an **exit** statement must be handled explicitly by a containing **except** statement with a handler of the form

when name , ... $\left[\,(\,\text{decl}\,,\,\dots\,)\,\right]$: body

As usual, the types of the expressions in the **exit** statement must equal the types of the variables declared in the handler. The handler must be an explicit one, i.e., exits to the implicit handlers of **resignal** statements or to the implicit *failure* handler enclosing a routine body are illegal.

The **exit** statement and the **signal** statement mesh nicely to form a uniform mechanism. The **signal** statement can be viewed simply as terminating a routine activation; an exit is then performed at the point of invocation in the caller. (Because this exit is implicit, it is not subject to the restrictions on exits listed above.)

The following is a simple example of the use of exits in search loops:

```
        elt: T
        begin
         for elt in array[T]$elements(x) do
           if special(elt) then exit found end
           end
         elt := make_new_one(...)   % Didn't find one, so make one up
         end except when found: end
         % At this point we have an object and we don't care how we got it
```

12.5 Example

We now present an example demonstrating the use of exception handlers. We will write a procedure, *sum_stream*, which reads a sequence of signed decimal integers from a character stream and returns the sum of those integers. The stream is viewed as containing a sequence of fields separated by spaces; each field must consist of a non-empty sequence of digits, optionally preceded by a single minus sign. *Sum_stream* has the following heading:

```
        sum_stream = proc (s: stream) returns (int) signals (sum_overflow,
                                                 integer_overflow(string),
                                                 bad_format(string))
```

Sum_stream signals sum_overflow if the sum of the numbers or an intermediate sum is outside the implemented range of integers. Integer_overflow is signalled if the stream contains an individual number that is outside the implemented range of integers. Bad_format is signalled if the stream contains a field that is not an integer.

We will use the *getc* operation of the *stream* data type (see Appendix III), whose type is

```
        proctype (stream) returns (char) signals (end_of_file, not_possible(string))
```

This operation returns the next character from the stream, unless the stream is empty, in which case end_of_file is signalled. Not_possible is signalled if the operation cannot be performed on the given stream (e.g., it is an output stream). We will assume that we are given a stream for which *getc* is always possible.

The procedure used to convert character strings to integers has the following heading:

```
        s2i = proc (s: string) returns (int) signals (invalid_character(char),
                                                 bad_format,
                                                 integer_overflow)
```

S2i signals invalid_character if its string argument contains a character other than a digit or a minus sign. Bad_format is signalled if the string contains a minus sign following a digit, more than one minus sign, or no digits. Integer_overflow is signalled if the string represents an integer that is outside the implemented range of integers.

An implementation of *sum_stream* is presented in Figure 5. There are two loops within an infinite loop: one to skip spaces, and one to accumulate digits for conversion to a number. Notice the placement of the inner end_of_file handler. If end_of_file is raised in the second inner loop, then the sum is computed correctly, and the first invocation of *stream$getc* will again raise end_of_file. This time, however, the infinite loop is terminated and execution transfers to the other end_of_file handler, which then returns the accumulated sum.

We have placed the remaining exception handlers outside of the infinite loop to avoid cluttering up the main part of the algorithm. Each of these exception handlers could also have been placed after the particular statement containing the invocation that signalled the corresponding exception. The (∗) form is used in the handler for the bad_format and invalid_character exceptions since the exception results are not used. Note that the overflow handler catches exceptions signalled by the **int$add** procedure, which is invoked using the

---

Fig. 5. The sum_stream procedure.

```
sum_stream = proc (s: stream) returns (int) signals (sum_overflow,
                                                      integer_overflow(string),
                                                      bad_format(string))
                sum: int := 0
                num: string
                while true do
                  % skip over spaces between values; sum is valid, num is meaningless
                  c: char := stream$getc(s)
                  while c = ' ' do
                    c := stream$getc(s)
                    end
                  % read a value; num accumulates new number, sum becomes previous sum
                  num := ""
                  while c ~= ' ' do
                    num := string$append(num, c)
                    c := stream$getc(s)
                    end
                    except when end_of_file: end
                  % restore sum to validity
                  sum := sum + s2i(num)
                  end
                  except when end_of_file: return(sum)
                         when integer_overflow: signal integer_overflow(num)
                         when bad_format, invalid_character (∗): signal bad_format(num)
                         when overflow: signal sum_overflow
                         end
                end sum_stream
```

infix + notation. Note also that in this example all of the exceptions raised by *sum_stream* originate as exceptions signalled by lower-level modules. Sum_stream simply reflects these exceptions upwards in terms that are meaningful to its callers. Although some of the names may be unchanged, the meanings of the exceptions (and even the number of results) are different in the two levels.

As mentioned above, we have assumed *stream$getc* never signals not_possible; if it does, then *sum_stream* will terminate, raising the exception

    failure("unhandled exception: not_possible")

13. Modules

A CLU program consists of a group of modules. Three kinds of modules are provided, one for each kind of abstraction we have found to be useful in program construction:

module ::= { equate } procedure
| { equate } iterator
| { equate } cluster

Procedures support procedural abstraction, iterators support control abstraction, and clusters support data abstraction.

A module defines a new scope. The identifiers introduced in the equates (if any) and the identifier naming the abstraction (the *module name*) are local to that scope (and therefore may not be redefined in an inner scope). Abstractions implemented by other modules are referred to by using non-local identifiers. The system must provide some means of determining what abstractions are meant by these non-local identifiers; one such mechanism is defined in Section 4.

The existence of an externally established meaning for an identifier does not preclude a local definition for that identifier. Within a module, any identifier may be used in a purely local fashion or in a purely non-local fashion, but no identifier may be used in both ways.

Example programs appear in Appendix IV.

13.1 Procedures

A procedure performs an action on zero or more *arguments*, and terminates returning zero or more *results*. A procedure supports a *procedural abstraction*: a mapping from a set of argument objects to a set of result objects, with possible modification of some of the argument objects. A procedure may terminate in one of a number of *conditions*; one of these is the *normal condition*, while others are *exceptional conditions*. Differing numbers and types of results may be returned in the different conditions.

The form of a procedure is

idn = **proc** [parms] args [returns] [signals] [where]
    routine_body
    end idn

where

args   ::= ([decl , ...])
returns   ::= **returns** (type_spec , ...)
signals   ::= **signals** (exception , ...)
exception   ::= name [(type_spec , ...)]
routine_body ::= { equate }
                   { own_var }
                   { statement }

In this section we discuss non-parameterized procedures, in which the *parms* and **where** clauses are missing. Parameterized modules are discussed in Section 13.4. Own variables are discussed in Section 13.5.

The heading of a procedure describes the way in which the procedure communicates with its caller. The *args* clause specifies the number, order, and types of arguments required to invoke the procedure, while the **returns** clause specifies the number, order, and types of results returned when the procedure terminates normally (by executing a **return** statement or reaching the end of its body). A missing **returns** clause indicates that no results are returned.

The **signals** clause names the exceptional conditions in which the procedure can terminate, and specifies the number, order, and types of result objects returned in each exception. In addition to the exceptions explicitly named in the **signals** clause, any procedure can terminate in the *failure* exception. The *failure* exception returns with one result, a string object. All names of exceptions in the **signals** clause must be distinct, and none can be *failure*.

A procedure is an object of some procedure type. For a non-parameterized procedure, this type is derived from the procedure heading by removing the procedure name, rewriting the formal argument declarations with one *idn* per *decl*, deleting the names of formal arguments, and finally, replacing **proc** by **proctype**.

As was discussed in Section 9.3, the invocation of a procedure causes the introduction of the formal variables, and the actual arguments are assigned to these variables. Then the procedure body is executed. Execution terminates when a **return** statement or a **signal** statement is executed, or when the textual end of the body is reached. If a procedure that should return results reaches the textual end of the body, the procedure terminates in the condition

    failure("no return values")

At termination the result objects, if any, are passed back to the invoker of the procedure.

The *idn* following the **end** of the procedure must be the same as the *idn* naming the procedure.

Examples of procedures are given in Section 13.3 and in Appendix IV.

13.2 Iterators

An iterator computes a sequence of *items*, one item at a time, where an item is a group of zero or more objects. In the generation of such a sequence, the computation of each item of the sequence is usually controlled by information about what previous items have been produced. Such information and the way it controls the production of items is local to the iterator. The user of the iterator is not concerned with how the items are produced, but simply uses them (through the **for** statement) as they are produced. Thus the iterator abstracts from the details of how the production of the items is controlled; for this reason, we consider an iterator to implement a control abstraction. Iterators are particularly useful as operations of data abstractions that are collections of objects (e.g., sets), since they may produce the objects in a collection without revealing how the collection is represented.

An iterator has the form

$$idn = \textbf{iter} \left[\text{parms} \right] \text{args} \left[\text{yields} \right] \left[\text{signals} \right] \left[\text{where} \right]$$
$$\text{routine\_body}$$
$$\textbf{end } idn$$

where

$$\text{yields} ::= \textbf{yields} \, (\, \text{type\_spec} \, , \, \dots \,)$$

In this section we discuss non-parameterized iterators, in which the *parms* and **where** clauses are missing. Parameterized modules are discussed in Section 13.4. Own variables are discussed in Section 13.5.

The form of an iterator is very similar to the form of a procedure. There are only two differences:

1. An iterator has a **yields** clause in its heading in place of the **returns** clause of a procedure. The **yields** clause specifies the number, order, and types of objects yielded each time the iterator produces the next item in the sequence. If zero objects are yielded, then the **yields** clause is omitted.

2. Within the iterator body, the **yield** statement is used to present the caller with the next item in the sequence. An iterator terminates in the same manner as a procedure, but it may not return any results.

An iterator is an object of some iterator type. For a non-parameterized iterator, this type is derived from the iterator heading by removing the iterator name, rewriting the formal argument declarations with one *idn* per *decl*, deleting the formal argument names, and finally, replacing **iter** by **itertype**.

An iterator can be invoked only by a **for** statement. The execution of iterators is described in Section 11.5.2.

An example of an iterator is

```
splits = iter (s: string) yields (string, string)
           for i: int in int$from_to(0, string$size(s)) do
             yield(string$substr(s, 1, i), string$rest(s, i + 1))
           end
         end splits
```

Additional examples of iterators are given in the next section and in Appendix IV.

Remarks

Iterators provide a useful mechanism for abstracting from the details of control. Furthermore, they permit **for** statements to iterate over the objects of interest, rather than requiring a mapping from the integers to those objects.

It is important to realize that the argument objects passed to the iterator are also accessible in the body of the **for** loop controlled by the iterator. If some argument object is mutable, and the iterator modifies it, the change can affect the behavior of the **for** loop body, and vice-versa. Such changes can be the cause of program errors.

As a general principle, an iterator should not modify its argument objects. There are some examples, however, where modification is appropriate. For example, an iterator that produces the characters from an input stream would advance the stream "window" (the currently accessible character) on each iteration.

Also as a general principle, the **for** loop body should not modify the iterator's argument objects. Again, examples exist where modification is desirable. In programming such examples, the programmer must ensure that the iterator will still behave correctly in spite of the modifications.

13.3 Clusters

A cluster is used to implement a new data type, distinct from any other built-in or user-defined data type. A data type (or data abstraction) consists of a set of objects and a set of primitive operations. The primitive operations provide the most basic ways of manipulating the objects; ultimately every action that can be performed on the objects must be expressed in terms of the primitive operations. Thus the primitive operations define the lowest level of observable object behavior.

The form of a cluster is

idn = **cluster** $\big[$ parms $\big]$ **is** idn , ... $\big[$ where $\big]$
       cluster_body
       end idn

where

cluster_body ::= $\big\{$ equate $\big\}$ **rep** = type_spec $\big\{$ equate $\big\}$
                    $\big\{$ own_var $\big\}$
                    routine $\big\{$ routine $\big\}$

routine   ::=   procedure
              $\big|$ iterator

In this section we discuss non-parameterized clusters, in which the *parms* and **where** clauses are missing. Parameterized modules are discussed in Section 13.4. Own variables are discussed in Section 13.5.

The primitive operations are named by the list of idns following the reserved word **is**. All of the idns in this list must be distinct.

To define a new data type, it is necessary to choose a *concrete representation* for the objects of the type. The special equate

     rep = type_spec

within the cluster body identifies *type_spec* as the concrete representation. Within the cluster, **rep** may be used as an abbreviation for *type_spec*.

The identifier naming the cluster is available for use in the cluster body. Use of this identifier within the cluster body permits the definition of recursive types (examples are given in Figures 6 and 7).

In addition to specifying the representation of objects, the cluster must implement the primitive operations of the type. The operations may be either procedural or control abstractions; they are implemented by procedures and iterators, respectively. Most of the routines in the cluster body define the primitive operations (those whose names are listed in the cluster heading). Any additional routines are *hidden*: they are private to the cluster and may not be named directly by users of the abstract type. All the routines must be named by distinct identifiers; the scope of these identifiers is the entire cluster.

Outside the cluster, the type's objects may only be treated abstractly (i.e., manipulated by using the primitive operations). To implement the operations, however, it is usually necessary to manipulate the objects in terms of their concrete representation. It is also convenient sometimes to manipulate the objects abstractly. Therefore, inside the cluster it is possible to view the type's objects either abstractly or in terms of their representation. The syntax is defined to specify unambiguously, for each variable that refers to one of the type's objects, which view is being taken. Thus, inside a cluster named T, a declaration

v: T

indicates that the object referred to by v is to be treated abstractly, while a declaration

w: **rep**

indicates that the object referred to by w is to be treated concretely. Two primitives, **up** and **down**, are available for converting between these two points of view. The use of **up** permits a type **rep** object to be viewed abstractly, while **down** permits an abstract object to be viewed concretely. For example, given the declarations above, the following two assignments are legal:

v := **up**(w)
w := **down**(v)

Only routines inside a cluster may use **up** and **down**. Note that **up** and **down** are used merely to inform the compiler that the object is going to be viewed abstractly or concretely, respectively.

A common place where the view of an object changes is at the interface to one of the type's operations: the user, of course, views the object abstractly, while inside the operation, the object is viewed concretely. To facilitate this usage, a special type specification, **cvt**, is provided. The use of **cvt** is restricted to the *args*, **returns**, **yields** and **signals** clauses of routines inside a cluster, and may be used at the top level only (e.g., **array[cvt]** is illegal). When used inside the *args* clause, it means that the view of the argument object changes from abstract to concrete when it is assigned to the formal argument variable. When **cvt** is used in the **returns**, **yields**, or **signals** clause, it means the view of the result object changes from concrete to abstract as it is returned (or yielded) to the caller. Thus **cvt** means abstract outside, concrete inside: when constructing the type of a routine, **cvt** is equivalent to the abstract type, but when type-checking the body of a routine, **cvt** is equivalent to the representation type.

The **cvt** form does not introduce any new ability over what is provided by **up** and **down**. It is merely a shorthand for a common case. In its absence, the heading of each routine would have to be written using the abstract type in place of **cvt**. Then inside the routine, additional variables of type **rep** would be declared, the argument objects assigned to these variables using **down**, and each **return**, **yield**, or **signal** statement would use **up** explicitly. The use of **cvt** simply causes the appropriate **up** or **down** to be performed automatically, and avoids the declaration of additional variables.

The type of each routine is derived from its heading in the usual manner, except that each occurrence of **cvt** is replaced by the abstract type.

Inside the cluster, it is not necessary to use the compound form (*type_spec$op_name*) for naming locally defined routines. Furthermore, the compound form cannot be used for invoking hidden routines.

The *idn* following the **end** of the cluster must be the same as the *idn* naming the cluster.

Some examples of clusters are shown in Figure 6. The first example implements (part of) a complex number data type. This data type may be implemented using either x and y coordinates, or rho and theta coordinates; the cluster shown uses x and y coordinates. Note that the *create*, *get_x*, and *get_y* operations might signal an exception if rho/theta coordinates were used; therefore these exceptions are listed in the headings, even though in this implementation the exceptions will not be signalled. The coordinates of a complex number can be queried using the *get* operations explicitly, or by using the special syntax, e.g.,

    a.theta

No *set* operations are provided, since complex numbers should be immutable like other numbers (integers, reals, etc.). Other operations on complex numbers are the usual arithmetic ones (only *add* is shown), and *equal*, *similar*, and *copy* (these are discussed in the remarks section below). (Note: we have assumed that *square_root* and *arctangent2* exist in the library.)

The second example cluster implements lists of integers. These lists are immutable, like pure lists in LISP. The implementation is recursive: the representation type refers to the abstract type. Notice the *elements* operation, which produces all integers in the list in order; it is an example of a recursive iterator.

The final example is sets of integers. The sets are mutable: operations *insert* and *delete* modify sets. Again note the *elements* iterator, which produces all elements of a set in some unspecified order. Also note the use of *is_in* in insert; since *is_in* requires an abstract object as its argument, **up** is used to provide one.

Remarks

The main reason CLU was developed was to support the use of data abstractions. Use of data abstractions leads to an object-oriented style of programming, in which concerns about data are primary and serve to organize program structure. It requires some effort to learn to program in this style, but the effort is worthwhile because the resulting programs are more modular, and easier to modify and maintain.

Fig. 6. Example Clusters

complex = **cluster is** create, add, get_x, get_y, get_rho, get_theta, equal, similar, copy

   rep = **struct**[x, y: **real**]

   create = **proc** (x, y: **real**) **returns (cvt) signals** (overflow, underflow)
        return(rep${x: x, y: y})
        end create

   add = **proc** (a, b: **cvt**) **returns (cvt) signals** (overflow, underflow)
      return(rep${x: a.x + b.x, y: a.y + b.y})
       resignal overflow, underflow
     end add

   get_x = **proc** (c: **cvt**) **returns (real) signals** (overflow, underflow)
        return(c.x)
        end get_x

   get_y = **proc** (c: **cvt**) **returns (real) signals** (overflow, underflow)
        return(c.y)
        end get_y

   get_rho = **proc** (c: **cvt**) **returns (real) signals** (overflow, underflow)
        return(square_root(c.x $\ast$ c.x + c.y $\ast$ c.y))
          resignal overflow, underflow
        end get_rho

   get_theta = **proc** (c: **cvt**) **returns (real) signals** (overflow, underflow)
          return(arctangent2(c.x, c.y))
            resignal overflow, underflow
          end get_theta

   % Note that the equal operation of the rep type tests equality of corresponding real
   % components, not identity of rep objects.

   equal = **proc** (c1, c2: **cvt**) **returns (bool)**
        return(c1 = c2)
        end equal

   similar = **proc** (c1, c2: **cvt**) **returns (bool)**
         return(c1 = c2)
         end similar

   copy = **proc** (c: complex) **returns** (complex)
        return(c)
        end copy

end complex

```
int_list = cluster is create, cons, car, cdr, is_in, is_empty, elements, equal, similar, copy

   rep = oneof[pair: pair,  empty: null]
   pair = struct[car: int,  cdr: int_list]

   create = proc () returns (cvt)
               return(rep$make_empty(nil))
            end create

   cons = proc (i: int, lst: int_list) returns (cvt)
               return(rep$make_pair(pair${car: i,  cdr: lst}))
            end cons

   car = proc (lst: cvt) returns (int) signals (empty)
            tagcase lst
              tag pair (p: pair): return(p.car)
              tag empty: signal empty
              end
            end car

   cdr = proc (lst: cvt) returns (int_list) signals (empty)
            tagcase lst
              tag pair (p: pair): return(p.cdr)
              tag empty: signal empty
              end
            end cdr

   is_in = proc (lst: cvt, i: int) returns (bool)
               while true do
                 tagcase lst
                   tag empty: return(false)
                   tag pair (p: pair): if p.car = i
                                         then return(true)
                                         else lst := down(p.cdr)
                                         end
                   end
                 end
               end is_in

   is_empty = proc (lst: cvt) returns (bool)
               return(rep$is_empty(lst))
               end is_empty
```

```
elements = iter (lst: cvt) yields (int)
        tagcase lst
          tag pair (p: pair): yield(p.car)
                              for i: int in elements(p.cdr) do
                                 yield(i)
                                 end
          tag empty:
          end
        end elements
```

% Note that the equal operation of the rep type tests equality of corresponding list
% elements, not identity of rep objects.

```
equal = proc(lst1, lst2: cvt) returns (bool)
        return(lst1 = lst2)
        end equal
```

```
similar = proc (lst1, lst2: cvt) returns (bool)
          return(lst1 = lst2)
          end similar
```

```
copy = proc (lst: int_list) returns (int_list)
       return(lst)
       end copy
```

```
end int_list
```

```
int_set = cluster is create, insert, delete, is_in, size, elements, equal, similar, copy

  rep = array[int]

  create = proc () returns (cvt)
           return(rep$new())
           end create

  insert = proc (s: cvt, i: int)
           if ~is_in(up(s), i)
              then rep$addh(s, i) end
           end insert
```

```
delete = proc (s: cvt, i: int)
            for j: int in rep$indexes(s) do
              if i = s[j]
                then s[j] := rep$top(s)
                       rep$remh(s)
                       return
                end
              end
            end delete


is_in = proc (s: cvt, i: int) returns (bool)
            for j: int in rep$elements(s) do
              if i = j
                then return(true) end
              end
            return(false)
            end is_in


size = proc (s: cvt) returns (int)
            return(rep$size(s))
            end size


elements = iter (s: cvt) yields (int)
                for i: int in rep$elements(s) do
                  yield(i)
                  end
                end elements


equal = proc (s1, s2: cvt) returns (bool)
            return(s1 = s2)
            end equal


similar = proc (s1, s2: int_set) returns (bool)
            if size(s1) ~ = size(s2)
              then return(false) end
            for i: int in elements(s1) do
              if ~is_in(s2, i)
                then return(false) end
              end
            return(true)
            end similar


copy = proc (s: cvt) returns (cvt)
            return(rep$copy(s))
            end copy


end int_set
```

A cluster permits all knowledge about how a data abstraction is being implemented to be kept local to the cluster. This localization permits the correctness of an implementation to be established by examining the cluster alone. Part of such a correctness proof involves showing that only legal representations are generated by the cluster. For example, in the *int_set* cluster above, not all arrays are legal *int_set* representations; only those without duplicate elements are legal. Information about what constitutes a legal representation is described during program verification by stating a *concrete invariant*. Each operation must preserve this invariant for each object that it manipulates of the abstract type. This requirement applies at all **return** and **signal** statements in operations, and also at **yield** statements in iterator operations.

When defining a new data type, it is important to provide a set of primitive operations sufficient to permit all interesting manipulations of the objects. There is no reason to attempt to define a minimal set, however; frequently used operations can be made operations of the cluster even if they could be implemented in terms of other operations.

Operations that will frequently be required are *equal*, *similar*, and *copy*. These operations are needed if the type being defined is intended for general use, since without these operations, the use of the type within another type's concrete representation is somewhat limited. For example, **array**[T]$copy cannot be used unless T has a *copy* operation. In addition, most types should provide I/O operations as discussed in Appendix III.

In many earlier sections, we have discussed the use of special syntactic forms for invoking operations, and have described how operations must be named and defined in order to make use of these syntactic forms. The use of such forms is quite unconstrained: the special form is translated to an invocation, and is legal if the invocation is legal.

Our reason for not imposing more syntactic constraints on operator overloading is that such constraints only capture a small part of what it means to use operator overloading correctly. For example, to overload " = " correctly, the *equal* operation should be an equivalence relation satisfying the substitution property; i.e., if two objects are *equal*, then one can be substituted for the other without any detectable difference in behavior. In the sections where special syntactic forms are described, we have discussed in each case what constitutes proper usage.

Overloading operator symbols is not the only place where care must be taken to ensure that the new definition agrees with common usage; the same care must be taken when redefining common operation names. For example, the *copy* operation should provide a "copy" of its argument object, such that subsequent changes made to either the old or the new object do not affect the other. In the case of an immutable type, like *complex_number* above, in which sharing between two objects will never be visible to the using program, *copy* can simply return its argument. Ordinarily, however, *copy* should copy its argument, including each component (using the *copy* operation of the component's type), as is done in the implementation of *int_set*.

The *equal* operation should return true if its two arguments are the same abstract object. This is necessary to satisfy the substitution property: if two objects are equal, then using one in place of the other in a computation will not alter the computation. Thus, implementing *equal* properly requires a thorough understanding of both the abstraction being implemented and the representation being used. Usually two mutable objects are equal only if they are the exact same object in the CLU universe; e.g., see *int_set$equal* above. For immutable objects, the contents of the object is usually all that matters; e.g., see *complex$equal* and *int_list$equal* above.

The *similar* operation should return true if its two arguments (both of the same type) have "equivalent state". This means that any query made about information in two similar objects immediately after they were determined to be similar would provide an equivalent answer for either of the two objects (i.e., the answers would be *similar*). Note that *similar* is a weaker condition than *equal*: two objects are *equal* if they are the *same* abstract object, and so of course they are *similar* for all time. *Equal* and *similar* return different results only for mutable types, because only mutable types have objects whose state can change. *Copy* and *similar* should be related as follows for any type T:

$$\forall\, x \in T \left[\, T\$similar(x, T\$copy(x)) \,\right]$$

Procedures defining operator symbols, *copy*, *similar*, and the I/O operations should never modify their arguments in a way that the user can detect. This rule does not prohibit "benevolent" side-effects, i.e., modifications that speed up future operations without affecting behavior in any other way.

13.4 Parameterized Modules

Procedures, iterators, and clusters may all be parameterized. Parameterization permits a set of related abstractions to be defined by a single module. Recall that in each module heading there is an optional *parms* clause and an optional **where** clause. The presence of the *parms* clause indicates that the module is parameterized; the **where** clause states certain constraints on permissible actual values for the parameters.

The form of the *parms* clause is

[parm , ...]

where

        parm ::=   idn , ... : type_spec
             | idn , ... : **type**

Each parameter is declared like an argument. However, only the following types of
parameters are legal: **int**, **real**, **bool**, **char**, **string**, **null**, and **type**. Parameters are limited to
these types because the actual values for parameters are required to be constants that can be
computed at compile-time. This requirement ensures that all types are known at
compile-time, and permits complete compile-time type-checking.

In a parameterized module, the scope rules permit the parameters to be used throughout
the remainder of the module. Type parameters can be used freely as type specifications, and
all other parameters can be used freely as expressions. For example, type parameters can be
used in defining the types of arguments and results:

        p = **proc** [t: **type**] (x: t) **returns** (t)

To use a parameterized module, it is first necessary to *instantiate* it; that is, to provide
actual, constant values for the parameters. (The exact forms of such constants are discussed
in Section 8.3.) The result of instantiation is a procedure, iterator, or type (where the
parameterized module was a procedure, iterator, or cluster, respectively) that may be used
just like a non-parameterized module of the same kind. For each distinct instantiation, (i.e.,
for each distinct list of actual parameters), a distinct procedure, iterator, or type is produced.

The meaning of a parameterized module is most easily understood in terms of rewriting.
When the module is instantiated, the actual parameter values are substituted for the formal
parameters throughout the module, and the *parms* clause and **where** clause are deleted.
The resulting module is a regular (non-parameterized) module. In the case of a cluster some
of the operations may have additional parameters; further rewriting will be performed when
these operations are used.

In the case of a type parameter, constraints on permissible actual types can be given in
the **where** clause. The **where** clause lists a set of operations that the actual type is required
to have, and also specifies the type of each required operation. The **where** clause constrains
the parameterized module as well: the only primitive operations of the type parameter that can
be used are those listed in the **where** clause.

The form of the **where** clause is

        where   ::=   **where** restriction , ...

where

```
restriction  ::=  idn has oper_decl , ...
              |   idn in type_set

oper_decl    ::=  op_name , ... : type_spec

op_name      ::=  name [ [ constant , ... ] ]

type_set     ::=  { idn | idn has oper_decl , ... { equate } }
              |   idn
```

There are two forms of restrictions. In both forms, the initial *idn* must be a type parameter. The **has** form lists the set of required operations directly, by means of *oper_decls*. The *type_spec* in each *oper_decl* must name a routine type. Note that if some of the type's operations are parameterized, particular instantiations of those operations must be given. The **in** form requires that the actual type be a member of a *type_set*, a set of types having the required operations. The two identifiers in the type_set must match, and the notation is read like set notation; e.g.,

{t | t **has** f: ... }

means "the set of all types *t* such that *t* **has** *f* ...". The scope of the identifier is the type_set.

The **in** form is useful because an abbreviation can be given for a type_set via an equate. If it is helpful to introduce some abbreviations in defining the type_set, these are given in the optional equates within the type_set. The scope of these equates is the type_set.

A routine in a parameterized cluster may have a **where** clause in its heading, and can place further constraints on the cluster parameters. For example, any type is permissible for the array element type, but the array *similar* operation requires that the element type have a *similar* operation. This means that **array**[T] exists for any type T, but that **array**[T]$similar exists only when T$similar exists. Note that a routine need not include in its **where** clause any of the restrictions included in the cluster **where** clause.

Two examples of parameterized clusters are shown in Figure 7. The first defines the *set* type generator. This cluster is similar to *int_set*, presented in the previous section. The main difference is that everywhere integer elements were assumed, now the parameter *t* is used. The *set* type generator has a **where** clause that requires the element type to provide an *equal* operation; in addition, the *similar* operation imposes an additional constraint on the element type by requiring a *similar* operation. Thus set[T] is legal if T has an *equal* operation; but set[T]$similar can be used only if T also has a *similar* operation. Note the procedure *is_in_sim*; it is a hidden routine of this implementation. Also note the use of the type_set *sim_type*.

Fig. 7. More Example Clusters

```
set = cluster [t: type] is create, insert, delete, is_in, size, elements,
                           equal, similar, similar1, copy, copy1
                     where t has equal: proctype (t, t) returns (bool)

  rep = array[t]
  sim_type = {s | s has similar: proctype (t, t) returns (bool)}

  create = proc () returns (cvt)
             return(rep$new())
             end create

  insert = proc (s: cvt, v: t)
             if ~is_in(up(s), v)
               then rep$addh(s, v) end
             end insert

  delete = proc (s: cvt, v: t)
             for j: int in rep$indexes(s) do
               if v = s[j]
                 then s[j] := rep$top(s)
                      rep$remh(s)
                      return
               end
             end
             end delete

  is_in = proc (s: cvt, v: t) returns (bool)
            for u: t in rep$elements(s) do
              if u = v
                then return(true) end
              end
            return(false)
            end is_in

  is_in_sim = proc (s: cvt, v: t) returns (bool)  where t in sim_type
                for u: t in rep$elements(s) do
                  if t$similar(u, v)
                    then return(true) end
                  end
                return(false)
                end is_in_sim

  size = proc (s: cvt) returns (int)
           return(rep$size(s))
           end size
```

```
elements = iter (s: cvt) yields (t)
              for v: t in rep$elements(s) do
                yield(v)
                end
              end elements

equal = proc (s1, s2: cvt) returns (bool)
          return(s1 = s2)
          end equal

similar = proc (s1, s2: set[t]) returns (bool)  where t in sim_type
          if size(s1) ~= size(s2)
            then return(false) end
          for u: t in elements(s1) do
            if ~is_in_sim(s2, u)
              then return(false) end
            end
          return(true)
          end similar

similar1 = proc (s1, s2: set[t]) returns (bool)
           if size(s1) ~= size(s2)
             then return(false) end
           for u: t in elements(s1) do
             if ~is_in(s2, u)
               then return(false) end
             end
           return(true)
           end similar1

copy = proc (s: cvt) returns (cvt)  where t has copy: proctype (t) returns (t)
         return(rep$copy(s))
         end copy

copy1 = proc (s: cvt) returns (cvt)
          return(rep$copy1(s))
          end copy1


end set
```

list = **cluster** [t: **type**] **is** create, cons, car, cdr, is_in, is_empty, elements, equal, similar, copy

```
rep = oneof[pair: pair,  empty: null]
pair = struct[car: t,  cdr: list[t]]

create = proc () returns (cvt)
          return(rep$make_empty(nil))
          end create

cons = proc (v: t, lst: list[t]) returns (cvt)
        return(rep$make_pair(pair${car: v,  cdr: lst}))
        end cons

car = proc (lst: cvt) returns (t) signals (empty)
       tagcase lst
         tag pair (p: pair): return(p.car)
         tag empty: signal empty
         end
       end car

cdr = proc (lst: cvt) returns (list[t]) signals (empty)
       tagcase lst
         tag pair (p: pair): return(p.cdr)
         tag empty: signal empty
         end
       end cdr

is_in = proc (lst: cvt, v: t) returns (bool)
                        where t has equal: proctype (t, t) returns (bool)
        while true do
          tagcase lst
            tag empty: return(false)
            tag pair (p: pair): if p.car = v
                                  then return(true)
                                  else lst := down(p.cdr)
                                  end
            end
          end
        end is_in

is_empty = proc (lst: cvt) returns (bool)
           return(rep$is_empty(lst))
           end is_empty
```

```
elements = iter (lst: cvt) yields (t)
             tagcase lst
               tag pair (p: pair): yield(p.car)
                                    for v: t in elements(p.cdr) do
                                       yield(v)
                                       end
               tag empty:
               end
             end elements


equal = proc (lst1, lst2: cvt) returns (bool)
                                where t has equal: proctype (t, t) returns (bool)
            return(lst1 = lst2)
            end equal


similar = proc (lst1, lst2: cvt) returns (bool)
                                 where t has similar: proctype (t, t) returns (bool)
              return(rep$similar(lst1, lst2))
              end similar


copy = proc (lst: cvt) returns (cvt)  where t has copy: proctype (t) returns (t)
            return(rep$copy(lst))
            end copy


end list
```

The *state* of a *set* object is the set of abstract objects currently in the set. What matters is the identity of the objects, not their state. This should help in understanding why *equal*, *similar*, and *copy* are written as they are. Notice that we have two new operations, *similar1* and *copy1*. *Similar1* returns true when two objects have equal state (in the abstract sense), whereas *similar* returns true when they have similar state. *Copy1* is to *similar1* what *copy* is to *similar*, i.e., T$similar1(x, T$copy1(x)) should always be true. In general, mutable type generators that behave like collections should provide *similar1* and *copy1* to ensure that types obtained from the generator can be used as part of the concrete representation of other types.

The second example is a *list* type generator, which is similar to *int_list* in the previous section. *List* does not place any constraints on its type parameter. Therefore any element type is permissible for lists, including type **any**. Note that types generated by the *list* type generator are immutable. The state of a list is considered to be the ordered set of objects in the list, where only the identity of the objects matters. Lists are immutable even if the objects in the lists are mutable, because the state of a list never changes.

Confusion can arise unless the designer and implementor of a data type have in mind a clear idea of exactly what constitutes the state of the objects of the type they are defining; it must be resolved in which cases it is only the identity of the components that matters, and in which cases their state matters as well.

The position taken in the *list* type generator above is that the state of a list consists only of the identity of the objects in the list, and does not depend on their state. Hence, these lists are immutable. This explains why *list* has no *similar1* or *copy1* operations, and why *equal*, *similar*, and *copy* are implemented as they are.

There are two restrictions on the kinds of constants that can be used in op_names of **where** clauses and type_sets. These restrictions eliminate certain ambiguities that would otherwise arise in type-checking. There is no need to understand or remember these restrictions, as the programs they affect are fairly bizarre, and should never occur in practice. The rules are included here solely for completeness.

The first restriction is that no type parameter, and no type identifier introduced in a type_set, can be used anywhere in an op_name constant. Thus, if *t* is a type parameter, an op_name of the form "compute[**array**[t]]" would be illegal. The second restriction deals with the way data abstractions depend on each other. If, in the interface of a data abstraction A, some data abstraction B is used in an op_name constant, we say that A is "restricted in terms of" B. We define *r-uses* to be the transitive closure of this relation. The second restriction, then, is that an abstraction cannot *r-use* itself.

13.5 Own Variables

Occasionally it is desirable to have a module that retains information internally between invocations. Without such an ability, the information would either have to be reconstructed at every invocation, which can be expensive (and may even be impossible if the information depends on previous invocations), or the information would have to be passed in through arguments, which is undesirable because the information is then subject to uncontrolled modification in other modules.

Procedures, iterators, and clusters may all retain information through the use of own variables. An own variable is similar to a normal variable, except that it exists for the life of the program, rather than being bound to the life of any particular routine activation. Syntactically, own variable declarations must appear immediately after the equates in a routine or cluster body; they cannot appear in bodies nested within statements. Own variable declarations have the form

> own_var ::= **own** decl
>
> | **own** idn : type_spec := expression
>
> | **own** decl , ... := invocation

Note that initialization is optional.

Own variables are created when a program begins execution, and they always start out uninitialized. The own variables of a routine (including cluster operations) are initialized in textual order as part of the first invocation of that routine, before any statements in the body of the routine are executed. Cluster own variables are initialized in textual order as part of the first invocation of the first cluster operation to be invoked (even if the operation does not use the own variables). Cluster own variables are initialized before any operation own variables are initialized.

Aside from the placement of their declarations, the time of their initialization, and their lifetime, own variables act just like normal variables and can be used in all the same places. As for normal variables, attempts to use uninitialized own variables (if not detected at compile-time) cause the run-time exception

> failure("uninitialized variable")

Own variable declarations in different modules always refer to distinct own variables, and distinct executions of programs never share own variables (even if the same module is used in several programs). Furthermore, own variable declarations within a parameterized module produce distinct own variables for each instantiation of the module. For a given instantiation of a parameterized cluster, all instantiations of the type's operations share the same set of cluster own variables, but distinct instantiations of parameterized operations have distinct routine own variables. For example, in the following cluster there is a distinct x and y for every type t, and a distinct z for every type-integer pair (t, i):

```
C = cluster [t: type] is ...
   ...
   own x: int := init(...) * 2

   P = proc (...)
       own y: ...
       ...
       end P

   Q = proc [i: int] (...)
       own z: ...
       ...
       end Q

   end C
```

Own variable declarations cannot be enclosed by an **except** statement, so care must be exercised when writing initialization expressions. If an exception is raised by an initialization expression, it will be treated as an exception raised, but not handled, in the body of the routine whose invocation caused the initialization to be attempted. This routine will then signal *failure* to its caller (see Section 12.2). In the example cluster above, if procedure P were the first operation of C[**string**] to be invoked, causing initialization of x to be attempted, then an *overflow* exception raised in the initialization of x would result in P signalling

```
failure("unhandled exception: overflow")
```

to its caller.

Remarks

Own variables are often useful in declaring "constants" that are either derived from complicated computations or are otherwise illegal in equates. In almost all such cases, the initialization can be attached directly to the declaration. For example,

```
own flip: complex := complex$create(0.0, 1.0)
own primes: sequence[int] := table_of_primes()
```

However, the data denoted by own variables may also change dynamically, and may contain history information, as the following (fairly useless) module demonstrates:

```
delayer = proc [t: type, delay: int] (x: t) returns (t) signals (not_yet)
            at = array[t]
            own oldies: at := at$new()
            at$addh(oldies, x)                    % add to waiting list
            if at$size(oldies) > delay            % if delayed long enough
              then oldies.low := 1                % prevent eventual overflow
                    return(at$reml(oldies))       % remove and return oldest
              else signal not_yet
            end
          end delayer
```

When cluster own variable initialization involves lengthy computations, one own variable can be initialized with an invocation of an (internal) operation, and the body of that operation can assign values directly to the other own variables:

```
C = cluster is ...
    ...
    own x: table := own_init()
    own y: table
    ...
    own_init = proc () returns (table)
                 ...
                 y := ...
                 ...
                 return(...)
               end own_init

end C
```

On occasion, when a particular program is known to use exactly one object of a particular user-defined type, it is tempting to implement the type such that the sole object is held by a cluster own variable. In this way, the object need not be passed as an argument to the various routines in the computation, many of which might not even use the object directly. This is a poor design decision in most cases, because the ways in which the type can be used later are then severely restricted. For example, the type cannot then be used in any program requiring several objects of that type. It is usually better to design types in as general a manner as possible.

With the introduction of own variables, procedures and iterators become potentially mutable objects. If the abstract behavior of a routine depends on history information (as does *delayer* above), then care must be exercised to guarantee that the routine is used correctly in other modules. (Ideally, a CLU system should have some method of controlling access to routines.) In general, own variables should not be used to modify the abstract behavior of a module.

Appendix I - Syntax

We use an extended BNF grammar to define the syntax. The general form of a production is:

         nonterminal ::= alternative
                       | alternative
                       | ...
                       | alternative

The following extensions are used:

         a , ...   a list of one or more *a*'s separated by commas: "a" or "a, a"
                      or "a, a, a" etc.
         {a}   a sequence of zero or more *a*'s: " " or "a" or "a a" etc.
         [a]   an optional *a*: " " or "a".

All semicolons are optional in CLU, but for simplicity they appear in the syntax as ";" rather than "[;]". Nonterminal symbols appear in normal face. Reserved words appear in bold face. All other terminal symbols are non-alphabetic, and appear in normal face.

module	::=	{ equate } procedure
		| { equate } iterator
		| { equate } cluster

procedure	::=	idn = **proc** [parms] args [returns] [signals] [where] ;
		        routine_body
		        end idn ;

iterator	::=	idn = **iter** [parms] args [yields] [signals] [where] ;
		        routine_body
		        end idn ;

cluster	::=	idn = **cluster** [parms] is idn , ... [where] ;
		        cluster_body
		        end idn ;

parms	::=	[parm , ...]
parm	::=	idn , ... : **type** | idn , ... : type_spec
args	::=	([decl , ...])

```
decl          ::=  idn , ... : type_spec

returns       ::=  returns ( type_spec , ... )

yields        ::=  yields ( type_spec , ... )

signals       ::=  signals ( exception , ... )

exception     ::=  name [ ( type_spec , ... ) ]

where         ::=  where restriction , ...

restriction   ::=  idn has oper_decl , ...
               |   idn in type_set

type_set      ::=  { idn | idn has oper_decl , ... ; { equate } }
               |   idn

oper_decl     ::=  op_name , ... : type_spec

op_name       ::=  name [ [ constant , ... ] ]

constant      ::=  expression
               |   type_spec

routine_body  ::=  { equate }
                   { own_var }
                   { statement }

cluster_body  ::=  { equate } rep = type_spec ; { equate }
                   { own_var }
                   routine { routine }

routine       ::=  procedure
               |   iterator

equate        ::=  idn = constant ;
               |   idn = type_set ;

own_var       ::=  own decl ;
               |   own idn : type_spec := expression ;
               |   own decl , ... := invocation ;
```

type_spec   ::=   **null**

             | **bool**

             | **int**

             | **real**

             | **char**

             | **string**

             | **any**

             | **rep**

             | **cvt**

             | **array** [type_spec]

             | **sequence** [type_spec]

             | **record** [field_spec , ...]

             | **struct** [field_spec , ...]

             | **oneof** [field_spec , ...]

             | **variant** [field_spec , ...]

             | **proctype** ([type_spec , ...]) [returns] [signals]

             | **itertype** ([type_spec , ...]) [yields] [signals]

             | idn [constant , ...]

             | idn

field_spec   ::=   name , ... : type_spec

statement   ::= decl ;

        | idn : type_spec := expression ;

        | decl , ... := invocation ;

        | idn , ... := invocation ;

        | idn , ... := expression , ... ;

        | primary . name := expression ;

        | primary [expression] := expression ;

        | invocation ;

        | **while** expression **do** body **end** ;

        | **for** [decl , ...] **in** invocation **do** body **end** ;

        | **for** [idn , ...] **in** invocation **do** body **end** ;

        | **if** expression **then** body
            { **elseif** expression **then** body }
            [**else** body]
            end ;

        | **tagcase** expression
            tag_arm { tag_arm }
            [**others** : body]
            end ;

        | **return** [(expression , ...)] ;

        | **yield** [(expression , ...)] ;

        | **signal** name [(expression , ...)] ;

        | **exit** name [(expression , ...)] ;

        | **break** ;

        | **continue** ;

        | **begin** body **end** ;

        | statement **resignal** name , ...

        | statement **except** { when_handler }
                    [others_handler]
                    end ;

tag_arm   ::= **tag** name , ... [(idn : type_spec)] : body

when_handler ::= **when** name , ... [(decl , ...)] : body

        | **when** name , ... (*) : body

others_handler ::= **others** [(idn : type_spec)] : body

body   ::= { equate }
                    { statement }

expression   ::= primary

                   | (expression)

Expression	%	precedence
~ expression	% 6	(precedence)
– expression	% 6	
expression ** expression	%	5
expression // expression	%	4
expression / expression	%	4
expression * expression	%	4
expression || expression	%	3
expression + expression	%	3
expression – expression	%	3
expression < expression	%	2
expression <= expression	%	2
expression = expression	%	2
expression >= expression	%	2
expression > expression	%	2
expression ~< expression	%	2
expression ~<= expression	%	2
expression ~ = expression	%	2
expression ~>= expression	%	2
expression ~> expression	%	2
expression & expression	%	1
expression **cand** expression	%	1
expression | expression	%	0
expression **cor** expression	%	0

primary	::=	**nil**
	|	**true**
	|	**false**
	|	int_literal
	|	real_literal
	|	char_literal
	|	string_literal
	|	idn
	|	idn [constant , ...]
	|	primary . name
	|	primary [expression]
	|	invocation
	|	type_spec $ { field , ... }
	|	type_spec $ [[expression :] [expression , ...]]
	|	type_spec $ name [[constant , ...]]
	|	**force** [type_spec]
	|	**up** (expression)
	|	**down** (expression)
invocation	::=	primary ([expression , ...])
field	::=	name , ... : expression

Reserved word: one of the identifiers appearing in bold face in the syntax. Upper and lower case letters are not distinguished in reserved words.

Name, idn: a sequence of letters, digits, and underscores that begins with a letter or underscore, and that is not a reserved word. Upper and lower case letters are not distinguished in names and idns.

Int_literal: a sequence of one or more decimal digits.

Real_literal: a mantissa with an (optional) exponent. A mantissa is either a sequence of one or more decimal digits, or two sequences (one of which may be empty) joined by a period. The mantissa must contain at least one digit. An exponent is 'E' or 'e', optionally followed by '+' or '–', followed by one or more decimal digits. An exponent is required if the mantissa does not contain a period.

Char_literal: either a printing ASCII character (octal value 40 through 176), other than single quote or backslash, enclosed in single quotes, or one of the following escape sequences enclosed in single quotes:

escape sequence	character
\'	' (single quote)
\"	" (double quote)
\\	\ (backslash)
\n	NL (newline)
\t	HT (horizontal tab)
\p	FF (newpage)
\b	BS (backspace)
\r	CR (carriage return)
\v	VT (vertical tab)
***	specified by octal value (exactly three octal digits)

The escape sequences may be written using upper case letters.

String_literal: a sequence of zero or more character representations, enclosed in double quotes. A character representation is either a printing ASCII character other than double quote or backslash, or one of the escape sequences listed above.

Comment: a sequence of characters that begins with a percent sign, ends with a newline character, and contains only printing ASCII characters and horizontal tabs in between.

Separator: a blank character (space, vertical tab, horizontal tab, carriage return, newline, form feed) or a comment. Zero or more separators may appear between any two tokens, except that at least one separator is required between any two adjacent non-self-terminating tokens: reserved words, identifiers, integer literals, and real literals.

Token: a sequence of printing ASCII characters representing a reserved word, an identifier, a literal, an operator, or a punctuation symbol.

Appendix II - Built-in Types and Type Generators

The following sections describe the built-in types and the types produced by the built-in type generators. For each type, the objects of the type are characterized, and all operations of the type are defined (with the exception of the encode and decode operations, which are defined in Appendix III, Section 8).

In defining an operation, *arg1*, *arg2*, etc., refer to the arguments (the objects, not the syntactic expressions), and *res* refers to the result of the operation. If execution of an operation terminates in an exception, we say the exception "occurs". By convention, the order in which exceptions are listed in the operation type is the order in which the various conditions are checked.

The definition of an operation consists of an *interface specification* and an explanation of the relation between arguments and results. An interface specification has the form

name: type_spec   side_effects
                    restrictions

If *side_effects* is null, no side-effects can occur. "PSE" (primary side-effect) indicates that the state of *arg1* may change. "SSE" (secondary side-effect) indicates that a state change may occur in some object that is contained in an argument. For operations of the built-in types, secondary side-effects occur when a subsidiary abstraction performs unwanted side-effects. (For example, side-effects are not expected when **array**[T]$similar invokes T$similar, but their absence cannot be guaranteed.) *Restrictions*, if present, is either a standard **where** clause, or a clause of the form

> **where each** T_i **has oper_decl**$_i$

which is an abbreviation for

> **where** T_1 **has oper_decl**$_1$, ..., T_n **has oper_decl**$_n$

Arithmetic expressions and comparisons used in defining operations are to be computed over the domain of mathematical integers or the domain of mathematical reals; the particular domain will be clear from context.

Definitions of several of the types will involve tuples. A tuple is written $\langle e_1, ..., e_n \rangle$; e_i is called the ith element. A tuple with n elements is called an n-tuple. We define the following functions on tuples:

$$\text{Size}(\langle e_1, ..., e_n \rangle) \equiv n$$
$$A = B \equiv (\text{Size}(A) = \text{Size}(B)) \wedge (\forall i \ s.t. \ 1 \leq i \leq \text{Size}(A))[a_i = b_i]$$
$$\langle a, ..., b \rangle \ || \ \langle c, ..., d \rangle \equiv \langle a, ..., b, c, ..., d \rangle$$

Front($\langle a, ..., b, c\rangle$) $\equiv$ $\langle a, ..., b\rangle$.

Tail($\langle a, b, ..., c\rangle$) $\equiv$ $\langle b, ..., c\rangle$

$\text{Tail}^0(A) \equiv A$ and $\text{Tail}^{n+1}(A) \equiv \text{Tail}(\text{Tail}^n(A))$

Occurs(A, B, i) $\equiv$ ($\exists$C,D)[(B = C $||$ A $||$ D) $\wedge$ (Size(C) = i $-$ 1)]

If Occurs(A, B, i) holds, we say that A occurs in B at index i.

II.1. Null

There is one immutable object of type **null**, denoted **nil**.

equal: **proctype (null, null) returns (bool)**
similar: **proctype (null, null) returns (bool)**

Both operations always return **true**.

copy: **proctype (null) returns (null)**

Copy always returns **nil**.

II.2. Bool

There are two immutable objects of type **bool**, denoted **true** and **false**. These objects represent logical truth values.

and: **proctype (bool, bool) returns (bool)**
or: **proctype (bool, bool) returns (bool)**
not: **proctype (bool) returns (bool)**

These are the standard logical operations.

equal: **proctype (bool, bool) returns (bool)**
similar: **proctype (bool, bool) returns (bool)**

These two operations return **true** if and only if both arguments are the same object.

copy: **proctype (bool) returns (bool)**

Copy simply returns its argument.

II.3. Int

Objects of type **int** are immutable, and are intended to model the mathematical integers. However, the only restriction placed on an implementation is that some closed interval [Int_Min, Int_Max] be represented, with **Int_Min** < 0 and **Int_Max** > 0. An overflow exception is signalled by an operation if the result of that operation would lie outside this interval.

add: **proctype (int, int) returns (int) signals (overflow)**
sub: **proctype (int, int) returns (int) signals (overflow)**
mul: **proctype (int, int) returns (int) signals (overflow)**

    The standard integer addition, subtraction, and multiplication operations.

minus: **proctype (int) returns (int) signals (overflow)**

    Minus returns the negative of its argument.

div: **proctype (int, int) returns (int) signals (zero_divide, overflow)**

    Div computes the integer quotient of *arg1* and *arg2*:
$$\exists r\ [(0 \leq r < |arg2|) \wedge (arg1 = arg2 \cdot res + r)]$$
    Zero_divide occurs if *arg2* = 0.

mod: **proctype (int, int) returns (int) signals (zero_divide, overflow)**

    Mod computes the integer remainder of dividing *arg1* by *arg2*. That is,
$$\exists q\ [(0 \leq res < |arg2|) \wedge (arg1 = arg2 \cdot q + res)]$$
    Zero_divide occurs if *arg2* = 0.

power: **proctype (int, int) returns (int) signals (negative_exponent, overflow)**

    This operation computes *arg1* raised to the *arg2* power. Power(0, 0) $\equiv 1$. Negative_exponent occurs if *arg2* < 0.

abs: **proctype (int) returns (int) signals (overflow)**

    Abs returns $|arg1|$, the absolute value of its argument.

max: **proctype (int, int) returns (int)**

    Max returns *arg1* if *arg1* $\geq$ *arg2*, otherwise it returns *arg2*.

min: **proctype (int, int) returns (int)**

    Min returns *arg1* if *arg1* $\leq$ *arg2*, otherwise it returns *arg2*.

from_to_by: **itertype (int, int, int) yields (int)**

> This iterator yields, in succession, *arg1*, *arg1* + *arg3*, *arg1* + 2*$arg3$, etc., as long as the value to yield, x, satisfies x $\leq$ *arg2* when *arg3* > 0, or *arg2* $\leq$ x when *arg3* < 0. The iterator continually yields *arg1* if *arg3* = 0. The iterator yields nothing when (*arg1* > *arg2*) $\wedge$ (*arg3* > 0) or when (*arg1* < *arg2*) $\wedge$ (*arg3* < 0).

from_to: **itertype (int, int) yields (int)**

> from_to(*arg1*, *arg2*) is equivalent to from_to_by(*arg1*, *arg2*, 1).

parse: **proctype (string) returns (int) signals** (bad_format, overflow)

> This operation computes the exact value corresponding to an integer literal. The argument must be an integer literal, with an optional leading plus or minus sign. Bad_format occurs if the argument is not of this form.

unparse: **proctype (int) returns (string)**

> Unparse produces an integer literal such that parse(unparse(*arg1*)) = *arg1*. Leading zeros are suppressed, and no leading plus sign is added for positive integers.

lt: **proctype (int, int) returns (bool)**
le: **proctype (int, int) returns (bool)**
ge: **proctype (int, int) returns (bool)**
gt: **proctype (int, int) returns (bool)**

> The standard ordering relations.

equal: **proctype (int, int) returns (bool)**
similar: **proctype (int, int) returns (bool)**

> These two operations return **true** if and only if both arguments are the same object.

copy: **proctype (int) returns (int)**

> Copy simply returns its argument.

II.4. Real

Objects of type **real** are immutable, and are intended to model the mathematical real numbers. However, only a subset of

$$D = [-Real\_Max, -Real\_Min] \cup \{0\} \cup [Real\_Min, Real\_Max]$$

need be represented, where 0 < Real_Min < 1 < Real_Max. Call this subset **Real**. We require that both 0 and 1 be elements of **Real**. If the exact value of a real literal lies in **D**, then the value in CLU is given by a function Approx, which satisfies the following axioms:

$$\forall\, r \in D \qquad\qquad \text{Approx}(r) \in \text{Real}$$
$$\forall\, r \in \text{Real} \qquad\quad\ \text{Approx}(r) = r$$
$$\forall\, r \in D - \{0\} \qquad \left|(\text{Approx}(r) - r)/r\right| < 10^{1-p}$$
$$\forall\, r,s \in D \qquad\qquad r \leq s \;\Rightarrow\; \text{Approx}(r) \leq \text{Approx}(s)$$
$$\forall\, r \in D \qquad\qquad\ \text{Approx}(-r) = -\text{Approx}(r)$$

The constant p is the *precision* of the approximation.

We define **Max_width** and **Exp_width** to be the smallest integers such that every non-zero element of **Real** can be represented in "standard" form (exactly one digit, not zero, before the decimal point) with no more than **Max_width** digits of mantissa and no more than **Exp_width** digits of exponent.

add: **proctype (real, real) returns (real) signals (overflow, underflow)**
sub: **proctype (real, real) returns (real) signals (overflow, underflow)**
mul: **proctype (real, real) returns (real) signals (overflow, underflow)**
minus: **proctype (real) returns (real)**
div: **proctype (real, real) returns (real) signals (zero_divide, overflow, underflow)**

These operations satisfy the following axioms:

1) $(a,b \geq 0 \lor a,b \leq 0) \;\Rightarrow\; \text{add}(a, b) = \text{Approx}(a + b)$
2) $\text{add}(a, b) = (1 + \varepsilon)(a + b) \qquad\qquad |\varepsilon| < 10^{1-p}$
3) $\text{add}(a, 0) = a$
4) $\text{add}(a, b) = \text{add}(b, a)$
5) $a \leq a' \;\Rightarrow\; \text{add}(a, b) \leq \text{add}(a', b)$
6) $\text{minus}(a) = -a$
7) $\text{sub}(a, b) = \text{add}(a, -b)$
8) $\text{mul}(a, b) = \text{Approx}(a \cdot b)$
9) $\text{div}(a, b) = \text{Approx}(a \,/\, b)$

In axiom 2, the value of p is the same as that used in defining Approx. Note that the infix and prefix expressions above are computed over the mathematical real numbers. The axioms only hold if no exceptions occur. An exception occurs if the result of an exact computation lies outside of **D**; overflow occurs if the magnitude exceeds **Real_Max**, and underflow occurs if the magnitude is less than **Real_Min**. Zero_divide occurs if *arg2* = 0.

power: **proctype (real, real) returns (real)**
                                  signals (zero_divide, complex_result, overflow, underflow)

This operation computes *arg1* raised to the *arg2* power. Zero_divide occurs if $(arg1 = 0) \land (arg2 < 0)$. Complex_result occurs if $arg1 < 0$ and *arg2* is non-integral. Overflow and underflow occur as explained above.

abs: **proctype (real) returns (real)**

Abs returns $\left|arg1\right|$, the absolute value of its argument.

max: **proctype (real, real) returns (real)**

Max returns *arg1* if *arg1* $\geq$ *arg2*, otherwise it returns *arg2*.

min: **proctype (real, real) returns (real)**

Min returns *arg1* if *arg1* $\leq$ *arg2*, otherwise it returns *arg2*.

i2r: **proctype (int) returns (real) signals** (overflow)

I2r returns a real number corresponding to the argument: *res* = Approx(*arg1*). Overflow occurs if *arg1* lies outside the domain **D**.

r2i: **proctype (real) returns (int) signals** (overflow)

R2i rounds to the nearest integer, and toward zero in case of a tie:
$$(|res - arg1| \leq .5) \wedge (|res| < |arg1| + .5)$$
Overflow occurs if the result lies outside the domain for CLU integers.

trunc: **proctype (real) returns (int) signals** (overflow)

Trunc truncates its argument toward zero: $(|res - arg1| < 1) \wedge (|res| \leq |arg1|)$. Overflow occurs if the result lies outside the domain for CLU integers.

exponent: **proctype (real) returns (int) signals** (undefined)

This operation returns the exponent that would be used in representing *arg1* as a literal in standard form: $res = \max\{i : |arg1| \geq 10^i\}$. Undefined occurs if *arg1* = 0.0.

mantissa: **proctype (real) returns (real)**

This operation returns the mantissa of *arg1* when represented in standard form:
$$res = \text{Approx}(arg1 / 10^{\text{exponent}(arg1)})$$
If r = 0.0 the result is 0.0.

parse: **proctype (string) returns (real) signals** (bad_format, overflow, underflow)

This operation computes the exact value corresponding to a real or integer literal, and then returns the result of applying Approx to that value. The argument must be a real or integer literal, with an optional leading plus or minus sign. Bad_format occurs if the argument is not of this form. Overflow occurs if the magnitude of the exact value of the literal exceeds **Real_Max**; underflow occurs if the magnitude is less than **Real_Min**.

unparse: **proctype (real) returns (string)**

Unparse produces a real literal such that parse(unparse(*arg1*)) = *arg1*. The general form of the literal is:

$$\left[-\right]i\_field.f\_field\left[e\pm x\_field\right]$$

Leading zeros in *i_field* and trailing zeros in *f_field* are suppressed. If *arg1* is integral and within the range of CLU integers, then *f_field* and the exponent are not present. If *arg1* can be represented by a mantissa of no more than **Max_width** digits and no exponent (i.e., $-1 \le$ exponent(*arg1*) $<$ **Max_width**), then the exponent is not present. Otherwise, the literal is in standard form, with **Exp_width** digits of exponent.

lt: **proctype (real, real) returns (bool)**
le: **proctype (real, real) returns (bool)**
ge: **proctype (real, real) returns (bool)**
gt: **proctype (real, real) returns (bool)**

The standard ordering relations.

equal: **proctype (real, real) returns (bool)**
similar: **proctype (real, real) returns (bool)**

These two operations return **true** if and only if both arguments are the same object.

copy: **proctype (real) returns (real)**

Copy simply returns its argument.

II.5. Char

Objects of type **char** are immutable, and represent characters. Every implementation must provide at least 128, but no more than 512, characters. Characters are numbered from 0 to some **Char_Top**, and this numbering defines the ordering for the type. The first 128 characters are the ASCII characters in their standard order.

i2c: **proctype (int) returns (char) signals** (illegal_char)

I2c returns the character corresponding to the argument. Illegal_char occurs if the argument is not in the range [0, **Char_Top**].

c2i: **proctype (char) returns (int)**

This operation returns the number corresponding to the argument.

lt: **proctype (char, char) returns (bool)**
le: **proctype (char, char) returns (bool)**
ge: **proctype (char, char) returns (bool)**
gt: **proctype (char, char) returns (bool)**

       The ordering relations consistent with the numbering of characters.

equal: **proctype (char, char) returns (bool)**
similar: **proctype (char, char) returns (bool)**

       These two operations return **true** if and only if the two arguments are the same object.

copy: **proctype (char) returns (char)**

       Copy simply returns its argument.

II.6. String

      Objects of type **string** are immutable. Each string represents a tuple of characters. The ith character of the string is the ith element of the tuple. There are an infinite number of strings, but an implementation need only support a finite number. Attempts to construct illegal strings result in a failure exception.

size: **proctype (string) returns (int)**

       This operation simply returns the size of the tuple represented by the argument.

empty: **proctype (string) returns (bool)**

       This operation returns **true** if and only if size($arg1$) = 0.

indexs: **proctype (string, string) returns (int)**

       If $arg1$ occurs in $arg2$, this operation returns the least index at which $arg1$ occurs:
          $res = \min\{i : \text{Occurs}(arg1, arg2, i)\}$
       Note that the result is 1 if $arg1$ is the 0-tuple. The result is 0 if $arg1$ does not occur.

indexc: **proctype (char, string) returns (int)**

       If $\langle arg1 \rangle$ occurs in $arg2$, the result is the least index at which $\langle arg1 \rangle$ occurs:
          $res = \min\{i : \text{Occurs}(\langle arg1 \rangle, arg2, i)\}$
       The result is 0 if $\langle arg1 \rangle$ does not occur.

c2s: **proctype (char) returns (string)**

       This operation returns the string representing the 1-tuple $\langle arg1 \rangle$.

concat: **proctype (string, string) returns (string)**

            Concat returns the string representing the tuple $arg1 \parallel arg2$.

append: **proctype (string, char) returns (string)**

            This operation returns the string representing the tuple $arg1 \parallel \langle arg2 \rangle$.

fetch: **proctype (string, int) returns (char) signals (bounds)**

            Fetch returns the $arg2^{th}$ character of $arg1$. Bounds occurs if $arg2 < 1$ or $arg2 > size(arg1)$.

rest: **proctype (string, int) returns (string) signals (bounds)**

            The result of this operation is $\text{Tail}^{arg2-1}(arg1)$. Bounds occurs if $arg2 < 1$ or $arg2 > size(arg1) + 1$.

substr: **proctype (string, int, int) returns (string) signals (bounds, negative_size)**

            If $arg3 \leq size(rest(arg1, arg2))$, the result is the string representing the tuple of size $arg3$ which occurs in $arg1$ at index $arg2$. Otherwise, the result is $rest(arg1, arg2)$. Bounds occurs if $arg2 < 1$ or $arg2 > size(arg1) + 1$. Negative_size occurs if $arg3 < 0$.

s2ac: **proctype (string) returns (array[char])**

            This operation places the characters of the argument as elements of a new array of characters. The low bound of the array is 1, and the size of the array is $size(arg1)$. The ith element of the array is the ith character of the string.

ac2s: **proctype (array[char]) returns (string))**

            Ac2s serves as the inverse of s2ac. The result is the string with characters in the same order as in the argument. That is, the ith character of the result is the $(i + low(arg1) - 1)^{th}$ element of the argument.

s2sc: **proctype (string) returns (sequence[char])**

            This operation transforms a string into a sequence of characters. The size of the sequence is $size(arg1)$. The ith element of the sequence is the ith character of the string.

sc2s: **proctype (sequence[char]) returns (string)**

            Sc2s serves as the inverse of s2sc. The result is the string with characters in the same order as in the argument. That is, the ith character of the result is the ith element of the argument.

chars: **itertype (string) yields (char)**

            This iterator yields, in order, each character of the argument.

lt: **proctype (string, string) returns (bool)**
le: **proctype (string, string) returns (bool)**
ge: **proctype (string, string) returns (bool)**
gt: **proctype (string, string) returns (bool)**

These are the usual lexicographic orderings based on the ordering for characters. The lt operation is equivalent to the following:

```
lt = proc (x, y: string) returns (bool)
    size_x: int := string$size(x)
    size_y: int := string$size(y)
    min: int
    if size_x <= size_y
      then min := size_x
      else min := size_y
      end
    for i: int in int$from_to(1, min) do
      if x[i] ~= y[i] then return(x[i] < y[i]) end
      end
    return(size_x < size_y)
    end lt
```

equal: **proctype (string, string) returns (bool)**
similar: **proctype (string, string) returns (bool)**

These two operations return **true** if and only if both arguments are the same object.

copy: **proctype (string) returns (string)**

Copy simply returns its argument.

II.7. Array Types

The **array** type generator defines an infinite class of types. For every type T there is a type **array**[T]. Arrays are mutable objects. The state of an object of type **array**[T] consists of:

     a) an integer Low, called the low bound, and
     b) a tuple Elts of objects of type T, called the elements.

We also define Size ≡ Size(Elts), and High ≡ Low + Size − 1. In defining various operations, Elts', High', etc. will be used to refer to the state just prior to invoking the operation. We want to think of the elements of Elts as being numbered from Low, so we define the *array_index* of the ith element to be (i + Low − 1).

For any array, Low, High, and Size must be legal integers. Any attempts to create or modify an array in violation of this rule results in a failure exception. Note that for all array operations, if an exception other than failure occurs, the states of all array arguments are <u>unchanged</u> from those at the time of invocation.

create: **proctype (int) returns (array[T])**

This operation returns a new array for which Low is *arg1* and Elts is the 0-tuple.

new: **proctype () returns (array[T])**

This is equivalent to create(1).

predict: **proctype (int, int) returns (array[T])**

Predict is essentially the same as create(*arg1*), in that it returns a new array for which Low is *arg1* and Elts is the 0-tuple. However, if *arg2* is greater than (less than) 0, it is assumed that at least |*arg2*| addh's (addl's) will be performed on the array. These subsequent operations may execute somewhat faster.

low: **proctype (array[T]) returns (int)**
high: **proctype (array[T]) returns (int)**
size: **proctype (array[T]) returns (int)**

These operations return Low, High, and Size, respectively.

empty: **proctype (array[T]) returns (bool)**

This operation returns **true** if and only if Size = 0.

set_low: **proctype (array[T], int)**   PSE

Set_low makes Low equal to *arg2*.

trim: **proctype (array[T], int, int) signals (bounds, negative_size)**   PSE

This operation makes Low equal to *arg2*, and makes Elts equal to the tuple of size min{*arg3*, High' – *arg2* + 1} which occurs in Elts' at index *arg2* – Low' + 1. That is, every element with array_index less than *arg2*, or greater than or equal to *arg2* + *arg3*, is removed. Bounds occurs if *arg2* < Low' or *arg2* > High' + 1. Negative_size occurs if *arg3* < 0. Note that this operation is somewhat like string$substr.

fill: **proctype (int, int, T) returns (array[T]) signals (negative_size)**

Fill creates a new array for which Low is *arg1* and Elts is an *arg2*-tuple in which every element is *arg3*. Negative_size occurs if *arg2* < 0.

fill_copy: **proctype (int, int, T) returns (array[T]) signals (negative_size)** SSE
where T **has** copy: **proctype (T) returns (T)**

This operation is equivalent to the following:

```
fill_copy = proc (nlow, nsize: int, elt: T) returns (at) signals (negative_size)
                                    where T has copy: proctype (T) returns (T)
              at = array[T]
              if nsize < 0 then signal negative_size end
              x: at := at$predict(nlow, nsize)
              for i: int in int$from_to(1, nsize) do
                at$addh(x, T$copy(elt))
                end
              return(x)
              end fill_copy
```

fetch: **proctype (array[T], int) returns (T) signals (bounds)**

Fetch returns the element of *arg1* with array_index *arg2*. Bounds occurs if *arg2* < Low or *arg2* > High.

bottom: **proctype (array[T]) returns (T) signals (bounds)**
top: **proctype (array[T]) returns (T) signals (bounds)**

These operations return the elements with array_indexes Low and High, respectively. Bounds occurs if Size = 0.

store: **proctype (array[T], int, T) signals (bounds)** PSE

Store makes Elts a new tuple which differs from the old in that *arg3* is the element with array_index *arg2*. Bounds occurs if *arg2* < Low or *arg2* > High.

addh: **proctype (array[T], T)** PSE

This operation makes Elts the new tuple Elts' || ⟨*arg2*⟩.

addl: **proctype (array[T], T)** PSE

This operation makes Low equal to Low' – 1, and makes Elts the tuple ⟨*arg2*⟩ || Elts'. Decrementing Low keeps the array_indexes of the previous elements the same.

remh: **proctype (array[T]) returns (T) signals (bounds)** PSE

Remh makes Elts the tuple Front(Elts'), and returns the deleted element. Bounds occurs if Size' = 0.

reml: **proctype (array[T]) returns (T) signals (bounds)** PSE

Reml makes Low equal to Low' + 1, makes Elts the tuple Tail(Elts'), and returns the deleted element. Incrementing Low keeps the array_indexes of the remaining elements the same. Bounds occurs if Size' = 0.

elements: **itertype (array[T]) yields (T)**

> This iterator is equivalent to the following:

> elements = **iter** (x: at) **yields (T)**
>   at = **array**[T]
>   **for** i: **int in** int$from_to(at$low(x), at$high(x)) **do**
>   **yield**(x[i])
>   **end**
>   **end** elements

indexes: **itertype (array[T]) yields (int)**

> This iterator is equivalent to **int**$from_to(**Low'**, **High'**).

equal: **proctype (array[T], array[T]) returns (bool)**

> Equal returns **true** if and only if both arguments are the same object.

similar: **proctype (array[T], array[T]) returns (bool)**   SSE
>   **where** T **has** similar: **proctype (T, T) returns (bool)**

> This operation is equivalent to the following:

> similar = **proc** (x, y: at) **returns (bool)**
>   **where** T **has** similar: **proctype (T, T) returns (bool)**
>   at = **array**[T]
>   **if** at$low(x) ~= at$low(y) **cor** at$size(x) ~= at$size(y)
>   **then return**(false)
>   **end**
>   **for** i: **int in** at$indexes(x) **do**
>   **if** ~T$similar(x[i], y[i]) **then return**(false) **end**
>   **end**
>   **return**(true)
>   **end** similar

similar1: **proctype (array[T], array[T]) returns (bool)**   SSE
>   **where** T **has** equal: **proctype (T, T) returns (bool)**

> Similar1 works in the same way as similar, except that T$equal is used instead of T$similar.

copy1:   **proctype (array[T]) returns (array[T])**

> Copy1 creates a new array with the same state as the argument.

copy: **proctype (array[T]) returns (array[T])**   SSE
             where T **has** copy: **proctype (T) returns (T)**

This operation is equivalent to the following:

```
copy = proc (x: at) returns (at) where T has copy: proctype (T) returns (T)
    at = array[T]
    x := at$copy1(x)
    for i: int in at$indexes(x) do
      x[i] := T$copy(x[i])
      end
    return(x)
    end copy
```

II.8. Sequence Types

The **sequence** type generator defines an infinite class of types. For every type T there is a type **sequence**[T]. An object of type **sequence**[T] consists of a tuple, **Elts**, of objects of type T, called the elements of the sequence. Sequences are immutable objects: a particular sequence always represents exactly the same tuple of objects. However, if the objects in the tuple are mutable, then the state of those objects may change.

For convenience, we define Size = Size(Elts). The elements of a sequence are numbered from 1 to Size. For any sequence, Size must be a legal integer; any attempt to create a sequence that violates this rule results in a failure exception.

new: **proctype () returns (sequence[T])**

    This operation returns the empty sequence.

size: **proctype (sequence[T]) returns (int)**

    This operation returns Size.

empty: **proctype (sequence[T]) returns (bool)**

    Empty returns **true** if and only if Size = 0.

subseq: **proctype (sequence[T], int, int) returns (sequence[T])**
                       signals (bounds, negative_size)

    If $arg3 \leq Size - arg2 + 1$ then the result is the tuple of size $arg3$ occurring in $arg1$ starting at index $arg2$. Otherwise, the result is the tuple $Tail^{arg2-1}(arg1)$. Bounds occurs if $arg2 < 1$ or $arg2 > Size + 1$. Negative_size occurs if $arg3 < 0$.

fill: **proctype (int, T) returns (sequence[T]) signals (negative_size)**

    Fill returns the sequence for which Elts is the $arg1$-tuple in which every element is $arg2$. Negative_size occurs if $arg1 < 0$.

fill_copy: **proctype (int, T) returns (sequence[T]) signals** (negative_size)   **SSE**
                    where T **has** copy: **proctype** (T) **returns** (T)

This operation is equivalent to the following:

fill_copy = **proc** (nsize: **int**, elt: T) **returns** (qt) **signals** (negative_size)
                                                where T **has** copy: **proctype** (T) **returns** (T)
                    qt = **sequence**[T]
                    if nsize < 0 **then signal** negative_size **end**
                    x: qt := qt$new()
                    for i: **int** in int$from_to(1, nsize) **do**
                      x := qt$addh(x, T$copy(elt))
                      end
                    return(x)
                    end fill_copy

fetch: **proctype (sequence[T], int) returns** (T) **signals** (bounds)

Fetch returns the $arg2^{th}$ element of *arg1*. Bounds occurs if *arg2* < 1 or *arg2* > **Size**.

bottom: **proctype (sequence[T]) returns** (T) **signals** (bounds)
top: **proctype (sequence[T]) returns** (T) **signals** (bounds)

These operations return the first and last elements of *arg1*, respectively. Bounds occurs if **Size** = 0.

replace: **proctype (sequence[T], int, T) returns (sequence[T]) signals** (bounds)

This operation returns a new sequence whose $arg2^{th}$ element is *arg3*, but which is otherwise the same as *arg1*. Bounds occurs if *arg2* < 1 or *arg2* > **Size**.

addh: **proctype (sequence[T], T) returns (sequence[T])**

Addh returns the sequence representing the tuple **Elts** || ⟨*arg2*⟩.

addl: **proctype (sequence[T], T) returns (sequence[T])**

Addl returns the sequence representing the tuple ⟨*arg2*⟩ || **Elts**.

remh: **proctype (sequence[T]) returns (sequence[T]) signals** (bounds)

Remh returns the sequence representing the tuple Front(**Elts**). Bounds occurs if **Size** = 0.

reml: **proctype (sequence[T]) returns (sequence[T]) signals** (bounds)

Reml returns the sequence representing the tuple Tail(**Elts**). Bounds occurs if **Size** = 0.

e2s: **proctype (T) returns (sequence[T])**

This operation returns the sequence representing the singleton tuple ⟨*arg1*⟩.

concat: **proctype (sequence[T], sequence[T]) returns (sequence[T])**

Concat returns the sequence representing the tuple *arg1* || *arg2*.

a2s: **proctype (array[T]) returns (sequence[T])**

This operation returns the tuple corresponding to the elements part of the state of *arg1*.

s2a: **proctype (sequence[T]) returns (array[T])**

This operation returns a new array with low bound 1 and with Elts as the elements part of the array state.

elements: **itertype (sequence[T]) yields (T)**

This iterator yields, in order, each element of Elts.

indexes: **itertype (sequence[T]) yields (int)**

This iterator is equivalent to int$from_to(1, Size).

equal: **proctype (sequence[T], sequence[T]) returns (bool)**   SSE
                  where T **has** equal: **proctype (T, T) returns (bool)**

Equal is equivalent to the following:

```
equal = proc (x, y: qt) returns (bool)
                    where T has similar: proctype (T, T) returns (bool)
        qt = sequence[T]
        if qt$size(x) ~= qt$size(y) then return(false) end
        for i: int in qt$indexes(x) do
          if x[i] ~= y[i] then return(false) end
          end
        return(true)
        end equal
```

similar: **proctype (sequence[T], sequence[T]) returns (bool)**   SSE
                  where T **has** similar: **proctype (T, T) returns (bool)**

Similar works in the same way as equal, except that T$similar is used instead of T$equal.

copy: **proctype (sequence[T]) returns (sequence[T])**   SSE
                 where T **has** copy: **proctype (T) returns (T)**

This operation is equivalent to the following:

copy = **proc** (x: qt) **returns** (qt) **where** T **has** copy: **proctype (T) returns (T)**
              qt = **sequence**[T]
              y: qt := qt$new()
              for e: T **in** qt$elements(x) **do**
                 y := qt$addh(y, T$copy(e))
                 end
              return(y)
              end copy

II.9. Record Types

The **record** type generator defines an infinite class of types. For every tuple of
name/type pairs $\langle(N_1, T_1), ..., (N_n, T_n)\rangle$, where all the names are distinct, in lower case, and in
lexicographic order, there is a type **record**$[N_1:T_1, ..., N_n:T_n]$. (However the user may write this
type with the pairs permuted, and may use upper case letters in names.) Records are mutable
objects. The state of a record of type **record**$[N_1:T_1, ..., N_n:T_n]$ is an n-tuple; the ith element of
the tuple is of type T_i. The ith element is also called the N_i-component.

create: **proctype** $(T_1, ..., T_n)$ **returns** (**record**$[N_1:T_1, ..., N_n:T_n]$)

           This operation returns a new record with the tuple $\langle arg1, ..., argN \rangle$ as its state.
           This operation is not available to the user; its use is implicit in the record
           constructor (see Section 10.8).

get_N_i: **proctype** (**record**$[N_1:T_1, ..., N_n:T_n]$) **returns** (T_i)

           This operation returns the N_i-component of the argument. There is a get_N_i
           operation for each N_i.

set_N_i: **proctype** (**record**$[N_1:T_1, ..., N_n:T_n]$, T_i)   PSE

           This operation makes the state of *arg1* a new tuple which differs from the old in that
           the N_i-component is *arg2*. There is a set_N_i operation for each N_i.

r_gets_r: **proctype (record[N_1:T_1, ..., N_n:T_n], record[N_1:T_1, ..., N_n:T_n])**   PSE

This operation changes the state of *arg1* to have the same components as *arg2*. It is equivalent to the following:

r_gets_r = **proc** (x, y: **record**[N_1:T_1, ..., N_n:T_n])
    x.N_1 := y.N_1
    ...
    x.N_n := y.N_n
    end r_gets_r

r_gets_s: **proctype (record[N_1:T_1, ..., N_n:T_n], struct[N_1:T_1, ..., N_n:T_n])**   PSE

This operation also changes the state of *arg1* to have the same components as *arg2*. It is just like r_gets_r, except that the new components come from a structure instead of a record.

equal: **proctype (record[N_1:T_1, ..., N_n:T_n], record[N_1:T_1, ..., N_n:T_n]) returns (bool)**

Equal returns **true** if and only if both arguments are the same object.

similar: **proctype (record[N_1:T_1, ..., N_n:T_n], record[N_1:T_1, ..., N_n:T_n]) returns (bool)** SSE
    where each T_i has similar: proctype (T_i, T_i) returns (bool)

Corresponding components of *arg1* and *arg2* are compared in (lexicographic) order, using T_i\$similar for the N_i-components. (The N_i-component of *arg1* becomes the first argument.) If a comparison results in **false**, the result of the operation is **false**, and no further comparisons are made. If all comparisons return **true**, the result is **true**.

similar1: **proctype (record[N_1:T_1, ..., N_n:T_n], record[N_1:T_1, ..., N_n:T_n]) returns (bool)** SSE
    where each T_i has equal: proctype (T_i, T_i) returns (bool)

Similar1 works in the same way as similar, except that T_i\$equal is used instead of T_i\$similar.

copy1:   **proctype (record[N_1:T_1, ..., N_n:T_n]) returns (record[N_1:T_1, ..., N_n:T_n])**

Copy1 returns a new record with the same state as the argument.

copy: **proctype (record[N_1:T_1, ..., N_n:T_n]) returns (record[N_1:T_1, ..., N_n:T_n])**   SSE
              where each T_i has copy: proctype (T_i) returns (T_i)

This operation is equivalent to the following (note that the N_i are in lexicographic order):

copy = **proc** (x: rt) **returns** (rt)
                    where T_1 **has** copy: **proctype** (T_1) **returns** (T_1),

                         ...
                         T_n **has** copy: **proctype** (T_n) **returns** (T_n)
              rt = **record**[N_1:T_1, ..., N_n:T_n]
              x := rt$copy1(x)
              x.N_1 := $T_1$$copy(x.N_1)

              ...
              x.N_n := $T_n$$copy(x.N_n)
              return(x)
              end copy

II.10. Structure Types

The **struct** type generator defines an infinite class of types. For every tuple of name/type pairs $\langle(N_1, T_1), ..., (N_n, T_n)\rangle$, where all the names are distinct, in lower case, and in lexicographic order, there is a type **struct**[N_1:T_1, ..., N_n:T_n]. (However the user may write this type with the pairs permuted, and may use upper case letters in names.) Structures are immutable objects. A structure of type **struct**[N_1:T_1, ..., N_n:T_n] is an n-tuple; the ith element of the tuple is of type T_i. The ith element is also called the N_i-component.

create: **proctype (T_1, ..., T_n) returns (struct[N_1:T_1, ..., N_n:T_n])**

This operation returns the structure representing the tuple $\langle arg1, ..., argN\rangle$. This operation is not available to the user; its use is implicit in the structure constructor (see Section 10.8).

get_N_i :   **proctype (struct[N_1:T_1, ..., N_n:T_n]) returns (T_i)**

This operation returns the N_i-component of the argument. There is a get_N_i operation for each N_i.

replace_N_i : **proctype (struct[N_1:T_1, ..., N_n:T_n], T_i) returns (struct[N_1:T_1, ..., N_n:T_n])**

This operation returns the tuple corresponding to arg1 with its N_i-component replaced by arg2. There is a replace_N_i operation for each N_i.

s2r: **proctype (struct[N_1:T_1, ..., N_n:T_n]) returns (record[N_1:T_1, ..., N_n:T_n])**

S2r returns a new record whose initial state is the tuple represented by the argument.

r2s: **proctype (record[N$_1$:T$_1$, ..., N$_n$:T$_n$]) returns (struct[N$_1$:T$_1$, ..., N$_n$:T$_n$])**

R2s returns the structure representing the tuple that is the current state of the argument.

equal: **proctype (struct[N$_1$:T$_1$, ..., N$_n$:T$_n$], struct[N$_1$:T$_1$, ..., N$_n$:T$_n$]) returns (bool)** SSE
where each T$_i$ has equal: proctype (T$_i$, T$_i$) returns (bool)

Corresponding components of *arg1* and *arg2* are compared in (lexicographic) order, using T$_i$\$equal for the N$_i$-components. (The N$_i$-component of *arg1* becomes the first argument.) If a comparison results in **false**, the result of the operation is **false**, and no further comparisons are made. If all comparisons return **true**, the result is **true**.

similar: **proctype (struct[N$_1$:T$_1$, ..., N$_n$:T$_n$], struct[N$_1$:T$_1$, ..., N$_n$:T$_n$]) returns (bool)** SSE
where each T$_i$ has similar: proctype (T$_i$, T$_i$) returns (bool)

Similar works in the same way as equal, except that T$_i$\$similar is used instead of T$_i$\$equal.

copy: **proctype (struct[N$_1$:T$_1$, ..., N$_n$:T$_n$]) returns (struct[N$_1$:T$_1$, ..., N$_n$:T$_n$])** SSE
where each T$_i$ has copy: proctype (T$_i$) returns (T$_i$)

This operation is equivalent to the following (note that the N$_i$ are in lexicographic order):

```
copy = proc (x: st) returns (st)
                where T₁ has copy: proctype (T₁) returns (T₁),
                        ...
                        Tₙ has copy: proctype (Tₙ) returns (Tₙ)
            st = struct[N₁:T₁, ..., Nₙ:Tₙ]
            return(st${N₁: T₁$copy(x.N₁),
                        ...
                        Nₙ: Tₙ$copy(x.Nₙ)})
        end copy
```

II.11. Oneof Types

The **oneof** type generator defines an infinite class of types. For every tuple of name/type pairs ⟨(N$_1$, T$_1$), ..., (N$_n$, T$_n$)⟩, where all of the names are distinct, in lower case, and in lexicographic order, there is a type **oneof[N$_1$:T$_1$, ..., N$_n$:T$_n$]**. (However the user may write this type with the pairs permuted, and may use upper case letters in names.) Oneofs are immutable objects. Each oneof represents a name/object pair (N$_i$, X), where X is of type T$_i$. For each object X of type T$_i$ there is a oneof for the pair (N$_i$, X). N$_i$ is called the tag of the oneof, and X is called the value.

make_N_i : **proctype** (T_i) **returns** $(oneof[N_1{:}T_1, ..., N_n{:}T_n])$

>This operation returns the oneof for the pair $(N_i, arg1)$. There is a make_N_i operation for each N_i.

is_N_i :   **proctype** $(oneof[N_1{:}T_1, ..., N_n{:}T_n])$ **returns (bool)**

>This operation returns **true** if and only if the tag of the argument is N_i. There is an is_N_i operation for each N_i.

value_N_i : **proctype** $(oneof[N_1{:}T_1, ..., N_n{:}T_n])$ **returns** (T_i) **signals (wrong_tag)**

>If the argument has tag N_i, the result is the value component of the argument. Wrong_tag occurs if the tag is other than N_i. There is a value_N_i operation for each N_i.

o2v: **proctype** $(oneof[N_1{:}T_1, ..., N_n{:}T_n])$ **returns** $(variant[N_1{:}T_1, ..., N_n{:}T_n])$

>This operation returns a new variant with an initial state that has the same tag and value as the argument.

v2o: **proctype** $(variant[N_1{:}T_1, ..., N_n{:}T_n])$ **returns** $(oneof[N_1{:}T_1, ..., N_n{:}T_n])$

>This operation returns the oneof with the same tag and value as the current state of the argument.

equal: **proctype** $(oneof[N_1{:}T_1, ..., N_n{:}T_n], oneof[N_1{:}T_1, ..., N_n{:}T_n])$ **returns (bool)**   SSE
                where each T_i **has equal: proctype** (T_i, T_i) **returns (bool)**

>If *arg1* and *arg2* have different tags, the result is **false**. If both tags are N_i, the result is that of invoking $T_i\$equal$ with the two value components.

similar: **proctype** $(oneof[N_1{:}T_1, ..., N_n{:}T_n], oneof[N_1{:}T_1, ..., N_n{:}T_n])$ **returns (bool)**   SSE
                where each T_i **has similar: proctype** (T_i, T_i) **returns (bool)**

>If *arg1* and *arg2* have different tags, the result is **false**. If both tags are N_i, the result is that of invoking $T_i\$similar$ with the two value components.

copy: **proctype** $(oneof[N_1{:}T_1, ..., N_n{:}T_n])$ **returns** $(oneof[N_1{:}T_1, ..., N_n{:}T_n])$ SSE
                where each T_i **has copy: proctype** (T_i) **returns** (T_i)

>If *arg1* represents the pair (N_i, X), then the result is the oneof for the pair $(N_i, T_i\$copy(X))$.

II.12. Variant Types

The **variant** type generator defines an infinite class of types. For every tuple of name/type pairs $\langle(N_1, T_1), ..., (N_n, T_n)\rangle$, where all of the names are distinct, in lower case, and in lexicographic order, there is a type **variant**$[N_1{:}T_1, ..., N_n{:}T_n]$. (However the user may write this type with the pairs permuted, and may use upper case letters in names.) Variants are mutable objects. The state of a variant consists of a name/object pair (N_i, X), where X is of type T_i. For each object X of type T_i there is a state (N_i, X). N_i is called the current tag of the variant, and X is called the current value.

make_N_i : **proctype** (T_i) **returns** (**variant**$[N_1{:}T_1, ..., N_n{:}T_n]$)

> This operation returns a new variant whose initial state is the pair $(N_i, arg1)$. There is a make_N_i operation for each N_i.

change_N_i : **proctype** (**variant**$[N_1{:}T_1, ..., N_n{:}T_n]$, T_i)   PSE

> This operation changes the state of *arg1* to be the pair $(N_i, arg2)$. There is a change_N_i operation for each N_i.

is_N_i :   **proctype** (**variant**$[N_1{:}T_1, ..., N_n{:}T_n]$) **returns** (**bool**)

> This operation returns **true** if and only if the current tag of the argument is N_i. There is an is_N_i operation for each N_i.

value_N_i : **proctype** (**variant**$[N_1{:}T_1, ..., N_n{:}T_n]$) **returns** (T_i) **signals** (wrong_tag)

> If the current tag of the argument is N_i, then the current value component is returned. Wrong_tag occurs if the current tag is other than N_i. There is a value_N_i operation for each N_i.

v_gets_v: **proctype** (**variant**$[N_1{:}T_1, ..., N_n{:}T_n]$, **variant**$[N_1{:}T_1, ..., N_n{:}T_n]$)   PSE

> This operation changes the state of *arg1* to have the same tag and value as *arg2*.

v_gets_o: **proctype** (**variant**$[N_1{:}T_1, ..., N_n{:}T_n]$, **oneof**$[N_1{:}T_1, ..., N_n{:}T_n]$)   PSE

> This operation also changes the state of *arg1* to have the same tag and value as *arg2*. It is just like v_gets_v, except that the new tag and value come from a oneof instead of a variant.

equal: **proctype** (**variant**$[N_1{:}T_1, ..., N_n{:}T_n]$, **variant**$[N_1{:}T_1, ..., N_n{:}T_n]$) **returns** (**bool**)

> This operation returns **true** if and only if *arg1* and *arg2* are the same object.

similar: **proctype (variant[N_1:T_1, ..., N_n:T_n], variant[N_1:T_1, ..., N_n:T_n]) returns (bool) SSE**
where each T_i has similar: proctype (T_i, T_i) returns (bool)

If *arg1* and *arg2* have different tags, the result is **false**. If both tags are N_i, the result is that of invoking T_i\$similar with the two value components.

similar1:   **proctype (variant[N_1:T_1, ..., N_n:T_n], variant[N_1:T_1, ..., N_n:T_n]) returns (bool) SSE**
where each T_i has equal: proctype (T_i, T_i) returns (bool)

If *arg1* and *arg2* have different tags, the result is **false**. If both tags are N_i, the result is that of invoking T_i\$equal with the two value components.

copy: **proctype (variant[N_1:T_1, ..., N_n:T_n]) returns (variant[N_1:T_1, ..., N_n:T_n])**   SSE
where each T_i has copy: proctype (T_i) returns (T_i)

If the current state of the argument is (N_i, X), then the result is a new variant whose initial state is (N_i, T_i\$copy(X)).

copy1:   **proctype (variant[N_1:T_1, ..., N_n:T_n]) returns (variant[N_1:T_1, ..., N_n:T_n])**

If the current state of the argument is (N_i, X), then the result is a new variant whose initial state is also (N_i, X).

II.13. Procedure and Iterator Types

Let A, R, L_1, ..., L_n be ordered lists of types, and let N_1, ..., N_n be distinct names in lower case and in lexicographic order. Then there is a type

proctype (A) returns (R) signals (N_1(L_1), ..., N_n(L_n))

and a type

itertype (A) yields (R) signals (N_1(L_1), ..., N_n(L_n)).

(The user may permute the N_i(L_i)'s, and may use upper case letters in names. If R is empty then "**returns (R)**" is not written, "(L_i)" is not written if L_i is empty, and "**signals (...)**" is not written if n = 0.)

The create operations are not available to the user; routines are created by compiling modules.

Let T be a procedure (or iterator) type in the following.

equal: **proctype (T, T) returns (bool)**
similar: **proctype (T, T) returns (bool)**

These operations return **true** if and only if both arguments are the same implementation of the same abstraction, with the same parameters.

copy: **proctype (T) returns (T)**

Copy simply returns its argument.

II.14. Any

The type **any** is the union of all types. There are no operations for the type **any**. Thus, for example, no **array[any]**$copy operation exists.

Appendix III - Input/Output

This appendix describes a set of standard "library" data types and procedures for CLU, provided primarily to support I/O. We do not consider this facility to be part of the language proper, but we feel the need for a set of commonly-used functions that have some meaning on most systems. This facility is minimal because we wish it to be general, i.e, to be implementable, at least in large part, under almost any operating system. The facility also provides a framework in which some other operations that are not always available can be expressed.

Some thought has been given to portability of programs, and possibly even data, but we expect that programs dealing with all but the simplest I/O will have to be written very carefully to be portable, and might not be portable no matter how careful one is.

The following additional types are described:

file_name - a naming scheme for files
stream - provides access to text files
istream - provides access to image files
date - calendar date and time

No type "file" exists, as will be explained.

III.1. Files

Our notion of file is a general one that includes not only storage files (disk files), but also terminals and other devices (e.g. tape drives). Each file will in general support only a subset of the operations described here.

There are two basic kinds of files, *text files* and *image files*. The two kinds of files may be incompatible. However, on any particular system, it may not be possible to determine what kind a given file is.

A text file consists of a sequence of characters, and is divided into lines terminated by newline ('\n') characters. A non-empty last line might not be terminated. By convention, the start of a new page is indicated by placing a newpage ('\p') character at the beginning of the first line of that page.

A text file will be stored in the (most appropriate) standard text file format of the local operating system. As a result, certain control characters (e.g. NUL, CR, FF, ↑C, ↑Z) may be ignored when written. In addition, a system may limit the maximum length of lines and may add (remove) trailing spaces to (from) lines.

Image files are provided to allow more efficient storage of information than is provided by text files. Unlike text files, there is no need for image files to be compatible with any local file format; thus, image files can be defined more precisely than text files.

An image file consists of a sequence of encoded objects. Objects are written and read using *encode* and *decode* operations of their types. (These in turn will call *encode* and *decode* on their components until built-in types are reached.) The objects stored in an image file are not tagged by the system according to their types. Thus, if a file is written by performing a specific sequence of *encode* operations, then it must be read back using the corresponding sequence of *decode* operations to be meaningful.

III.2. File Names

File names are immutable objects used to name files. The system file name format is viewed as consisting of four string components:

directory - specifies a file directory or device
name   -   the primary name of the file (e.g. "thesis")
suffix -   a name normally indicating the type of file (e.g. "clu" for a
            CLU source file)
other   -   all other components of the system file name form

The *directory* and *other* components may have internal syntax. The *name* and *suffix* should be short identifiers. (For example, in the TOPS-20 file name "ps:⟨cluser⟩ref.lpt.3", the *directory* is "ps:⟨cluser⟩", the *name* is "ref", the *suffix* is "lpt", and the *other* is "3". In the UNIX path name "/usr/snyder/doc/refman.r", the *directory* is "/usr/snyder/doc", the *name* is "refman", the *suffix* is "r", and there is no *other*.

A null component has the following interpretation:

directory - denotes the current "working" directory. (For example, the
            "connected directory" under TOPS-20 and the "current
            directory" under UNIX. See also Section 9 of this
            appendix.)
name   -   may be illegal, have a unique interpretation, or be ignored.
            (For example, under TOPS-20, a null name is illegal for
            most directories, but for some devices, the name is
            ignored.)
suffix -   may be illegal, have a unique interpretation, or be ignored.
            (For example, under TOPS-20, a null suffix is legal, as in
            "⟨rws⟩foo".)
other   -   should imply a reasonable default.

The operations on file names are:

create: **proctype (string, string, string, string) returns** (file_name)
                                              signals (bad_format)

> This operation creates a file name from its components. *Arg1* is the directory part, *arg2* is the name part, *arg3* is the suffix part, and *arg4* is the other part for the new file_name. In the process of creating a file name, the string arguments may be transformed, e.g. by truncation or case-conversion.

get_dir: **proctype** (file_name) **returns (string)**
get_name: **proctype** (file_name) **returns (string)**
get_suffix: **proctype** (file_name) **returns (string)**
get_other: **proctype** (file_name) **returns (string)**

> These operations return string forms of the components of a file name. If the file name was created using the *create* operation, then the strings returned may be different than those given as arguments to *create*, e.g., they may be truncated or case-converted.

parse: **proctype (string) returns** (file_name) **signals** (bad_format)

> This operation creates a file name given a string in the system standard file name syntax.

unparse: **proctype** (file_name) **returns (string)**

> This operation transforms a file name into the system standard file name syntax. We require that
>   parse(unparse(fn)) = fn
>   create(fn.dir, fn.name, fn.suffix, fn.other) = fn
> for all file names *fn*. One implication of this rule is that there can be no file name that can be created by *create* but not by *parse*; if a system does have file names that have no string representation in the system standard file name syntax, then *create* must reject those file names as having a bad format. Alternatively, the file name syntax can be extended so that it can express all possible file names.

make_output: **proctype** (file_name, **string) returns** (file_name) **signals** (bad_format)

> This operation is used by programs that take input from a file and write new files whose names are based on the input file name. The operation transforms the file name into one that is suitable for an output file. The transformation is done as follows: (1) the suffix is set to the given suffix (*arg2*); (2) if the old directory is not suitable for writing, then it is set to null; (3) the name, if null and meaningless, is set to "output". (Examples of directories that may not be suitable for writing are directories that involve transferring files over a slow network.)

make_temp: **proctype (string, string, string) returns** (file_name) **signals** (bad_format)

This operation creates a file name appropriate for a temporary file, using the given preferred directory name (*arg1*), program name (*arg2*), and file identifier (*arg3*). To be useful, both the program name and the file identifier should be short and alphabetic. The returned file name, when used as an argument to *stream$open* or *istream$open* to open a new file for writing, is guaranteed to create a new file, and will not overwrite an existing file. Further file name references to the created file should be made using the name returned by the stream or istream *get_name* operation.

equal: **proctype** (file_name, file_name) **returns (bool)**

Returns **true** if and only if the two file_names will *unparse* to equal strings.

similar: **proctype** (file_name, file_name) **returns (bool)**

The same as the equal operation.

copy: **proctype** (file_name) **returns** (file_name)

Copy simply returns its argument.

III.3. A File Type?

Although files are the basic information-containing objects in this package, we do not recommend that a file type be introduced. The reason for this recommendation is that few systems provide an adequate representation for files.

On many systems, the most reliable representation of a file (accessible to the user) is a channel (stream) to that file. However, this representation is inappropriate for a CLU file type, since possession of a channel to a file often implies locking that file.

Another possible representation is a file name. However, file names are one level indirect from files, via the file directory. As a result, the relationship of a file name to a file object is time-varying. Using file names as a representation for files would imply that all file operations could signal *non_existent_file*.

Therefore, operations related to file objects are performed by two clusters, *stream* and *istream*, and operations related to the directory system are performed by procedures.

Note that two opens for read with the same file name might return streams to two different files. We cannot guarantee anything about what may happen to a file after a program obtains a stream to it.

III.4. Streams

Streams provide the means to read and write text files, and to perform some other operations on file objects. The operations allowed on any particular stream depend upon the access mode. In addition, certain operations may have no effect in some implementations.

When an operation cannot be performed, because of an incorrect access mode, because of implementation limitations, or because of properties of an individual file or device, then the operation will signal *not_possible* (unless the description of the operation explicitly says that the invocation will be ignored).

The PSE and SSE indicators used in the previous appendix will not be used here; in many cases the exact form (and time) of change depends on the particular operating system.

open: **proctype** (file_name, **string**) **returns** (stream) **signals** (not_possible(**string**))

The possible access modes (*arg2*) are "read", "write", and "append". If *arg2* is not one of these strings, not_possible("bad access mode") is signalled. In those cases where the system is able to detect that the specified pre-existing file is not a text file, not_possible("wrong file type") is signalled.

If the mode is "read", then the named file must exist. If the file exists, a stream is returned upon which input operations can be performed.

If the mode is "write", a new file is created or an old file is rewritten. A stream is returned upon which output operations can be performed. Write mode to storage files should guarantee exclusive access to the file, if possible.

If the mode is "append", then if the named file does not exist, one is created. A stream is returned, positioned at the end of the file, upon which output operations can be performed. Append mode to storage files should guarantee exclusive access to the file, if possible.

primary_input: **proctype** () **returns** (stream)

This operation returns the "primary" input stream, suitable for reading. This is usually a stream to the user's terminal, but may be set by the operating system.

primary_output: **proctype** () **returns** (stream)

This operation returns the "primary" output stream, suitable for writing. This is usually a stream to the user's terminal, but may be set by the operating system.

error_output: **proctype** () **returns** (stream)

This operation returns the "primary" output stream for error messages, suitable for writing. This is usually a stream to the user's terminal, but may be set by the operating system.

can_read: **proctype** (stream) **returns (bool)**

                 Can_read returns **true** if input operations appear possible on the stream.

can_write: **proctype** (stream) **returns (bool)**

                 Can_write returns **true** if output operations appear possible on the stream.

getc: **proctype** (stream) **returns (char) signals** (end_of_file, not_possible(**string**))

                 This input operation removes the next character from the stream and returns it.

peekc: **proctype** (stream) **returns (char) signals** (end_of_file, not_possible(**string**))

                 This input operation is like *getc*, except that the character is not removed from the stream.

empty: **proctype** (stream) **returns (bool) signals** (not_possible(**string**))

                 This input operation returns **true** if and only if there are no more characters in the stream. It is equivalent to an invocation of *peekc*, where **true** is returned if *peekc* returns a character and **false** is returned if *peekc* signals end_of_file. Thus in the case of terminals, for example, this operation may wait until additional characters have been typed by the user.

putc: **proctype** (stream, **char**) **signals** (not_possible(**string**))

                 This output operation appends the given character to the stream. Writing a newline indicates the end of the current line.

putc_image: **proctype** (stream, **char**) **signals** (not_possible(**string**))

                 This output operation is like *putc*, except that an arbitrary character may be written and the character is not interpreted by the CLU I/O system. (For example, the ITS XGP program expects a text file containing certain escape sequences. An escape sequence consists of a special character followed by a fixed number of arbitrary characters. These characters could be the same as an end-of-line mark, but they are recognized as data by their context. On a record-oriented system, such characters would be part of the data. In either case, writing a newline in image mode would not be interpreted by the CLU system as indicating an end-of-line.) Characters written to a terminal stream with this operation can be used to cause terminal-dependent control functions.

getc_image: **proctype** (stream) **returns (char) signals** (end_of_file, not_possible(**string**))

                 This input operation is provided to read escape sequences in text files, as might be written using *putc_image*. Using this operation inhibits the recognition of end-of-line marks, where used. When reading from a terminal stream, the character is not echoed and is not subject to interpretation as an editing command.

get_lineno: **proctype** (stream) **returns (int) signals** (end_of_file, not_possible(**string**))

This input operation returns the line number of the current (being or about to be read) line. If the system maintains explicit line numbers in the file, said line numbers are returned. Otherwise, lines are implicitly numbered, starting with 1.

set_lineno: **proctype** (stream, **int**) **signals** (not_possible(**string**))

If the system maintains explicit line numbers in the file, this output operation sets the line number of the next (not yet started) line. Otherwise, it is ignored.

reset: **proctype** (stream) **signals** (not_possible(**string**))

This operation resets the stream so that the next input or output operation will read or write the first character in the file. The line number is reset to its initial value. The end-of-file status is cleared on a terminal stream.

flush: **proctype** (stream) **signals** (not_possible(**string**))

Any buffered output is written to the file, if possible. This operation should be used for streams that record the progress of a program. It can be used to maximize the amount of recorded status visible to the user or available in case the program terminates prematurely.

get_line_length: **proctype** (stream) **returns (int) signals** (no_limit)

If the file or device to which the stream is attached has a natural maximum line length, then that length is returned. Otherwise, no_limit is signalled. The line length does not include newline characters.

get_page_length: **proctype** (stream) **returns (int) signals** (no_limit)

If the device to which the stream is attached has a natural maximum page length, then that length is returned. Otherwise, no_limit is signalled. Storage files will generally not have page lengths.

get_date: **proctype** (stream) **returns** (date) **signals** (not_possible(**string**))

This operation returns the date of the last modification of the corresponding storage file.

set_date: **proctype** (stream, date) **signals** (not_possible(**string**))

This operation sets the modification date of the corresponding storage file. The modification date is set automatically when a file is opened in "write" or "append" mode.

get_name: **proctype** (stream) **returns** (file_name) **signals** (not_possible(**string**))

This operation returns the name of the corresponding file. It may be different than the name used to open the file, in that defaults have been resolved and link indirections have been followed.

close: **proctype** (stream) **signals** (not_possible(**string**))

This operation attempts to terminate I/O and remove the association between the stream and the file. If successful, further use of operations that signal not_possible will signal not_possible. This operation will fail if buffered output cannot be written.

abort: **proctype** (stream)

This operation always terminates I/O and removes the association between the stream and the file. If buffered output cannot be written, it will be lost, and if a new file was being written, the file may or may not exist.

is_closed: **proctype** (stream) **returns** (**bool**)

This operation returns **true** if and only if the stream is closed.

is_terminal: **proctype** (stream) **returns** (**bool**)

This operation returns **true** if and only if the stream is attached to an interactive terminal (see Section 6 of this appendix).

getl: **proctype** (stream) **returns** (**string**)
                              signals (end_of_file, not_possible(**string**))

This input operation reads and returns (the remainder of) the current input line and reads but does not return the terminating newline (if any). This operation signals end_of_file only if there were no characters and end-of-file was detected.

putl: **proctype** (stream, **string**) **signals** (not_possible(**string**))

This output operation writes the characters of the string onto the stream, followed by a newline.

gets: **proctype** (stream, **string**) **returns** (**string**)
                              signals (end_of_file, not_possible(**string**))

This input operation reads characters until a terminating character (one in *arg2*) or end-of-file is seen. The characters up to the terminator are returned; the terminator (if any) is left in the stream. This operation signals end_of_file only if there were no characters and end-of-file was detected.

gets_image: **proctype** (stream, **string**) **returns** (**string**)
                        signals (end_of_file, not_possible(**string**))

This input operation reads characters until a terminating character (one in *arg2*) or end-of-file is seen. Using this operation inhibits the recognition of end-of-line marks, where used. When reading from a terminal stream, the characters read are not echoed and are not subject to interpretation as editing commands. The characters up to the terminator are returned; the terminator (if any) is left in the stream. This operation signals end_of_file only if there were no characters and end-of-file was detected.

puts: **proctype** (stream, **string**) **signals** (not_possible(**string**))

This output operation simply writes the characters in the string using *putc*. Naturally it may be somewhat more efficient than doing a series of individual *putc*'s.

puts_image: **proctype** (stream, **string**) **signals** (not_possible(**string**))

This output operation simply writes the characters in the string using *putc_image*. Naturally it may be somewhat more efficient than doing a series of individual *putc_image*'s.

putzero: **proctype** (stream, **string**, **int**)
                      signals (negative_field_width, not_possible(**string**))

Outputs the string. However, if the length of the string is less than the field width (*arg3*), then the appropriate number of extra zeros before the first digit or '.' in the string (or at the end, if no such characters) are also output.

putleft: **proctype** (stream, **string**, **int**)
                      signals (negative_field_width, not_possible(**string**))

Outputs the string. However, if the length of the string is less than *arg3*, then the appropriate number of extra spaces after the string are also output.

putright: **proctype** (stream, **string**, **int**)
                      signals (negative_field_width, not_possible(**string**))

Outputs the string. However, if the length of the string is less than *arg3*, then the appropriate number of extra spaces before the string are also output.

putspace: **proctype** (stream, **int**) **signals** (negative_field_width, not_possible(**string**))

This operation outputs *arg2* spaces.

set_output_buffered: **proctype** (stream, **bool**) **signals** (not_possible(**string**))

> This operation sets the output buffering mode. Normally, output may be arbitrarily buffered before it is actually written out. Unbuffered output can be used on some systems to decrease the amount of information lost if the program terminates prematurely. For terminal streams, unbuffered output is useful in programs that output incomplete lines as they are working, to allow the user to watch the progress of the program.

get_output_buffered: **proctype** (stream) **returns** (**bool**)

> This operation returns **true** if and only if output to the stream is being buffered.

equal: **proctype** (stream, stream) **returns** (**bool**)

> Returns **true** if and only if both arguments are the same stream.

similar: **proctype** (stream, stream) **returns** (**bool**)

> Returns **true** if and only both arguments are the same stream.

copy: **proctype** (stream) **returns** (stream)

> Returns its argument.

III.5. String I/O

It is occasionally useful to be able to construct a stream that, rather than being connected to a file, instead simply collects the output text into a string. Conversely, it is occasionally useful to be able to take a string and convert it into an input stream so that it can be given to a procedure that expects a stream. String streams allow these functions to be performed. A string stream does not have a file name, a creation date, a maximum line or page length, or explicit line numbers. The following stream operations deal with string streams:

create_input: **proctype (string) returns** (stream)

> An input stream is created that will return the characters in the given string. If the string is non-empty and does not end with a newline, then an extra terminating newline will be appended to the string.

create_output: **proctype () returns** (stream)

> An output stream is created that will collect output text in an internal buffer. The text may be extracted using the *get_contents* operation.

get_contents: **proctype** (stream) **returns** (**string**) **signals** (not_possible(**string**))

> This operation returns the text that has so far been output to a string stream. It
> will signal not_possible if the stream was not created by *create_output*.

III.6. Terminal I/O

Terminal I/O is performed via streams attached to interactive terminals. Such a stream is
normally obtained via the *primary_input* and *primary_output* operations. A terminal stream is
capable of performing both input and output operations. A number of additional operations
are possible on terminal streams, and a number of standard operations have special
interpretations.

Terminal input will normally be buffered so that the user may perform editing functions,
such as deleting the last character on the current line, deleting the current line, redisplaying
the current line, and redisplaying the current line after clearing the screen. Specific
characters for causing these functions are not suggested. In addition, some means must be
provided for the user to indicate end-of-file, so that a terminal stream can be given to a
program that expects an arbitrary stream and reads it until end-of-file. The end-of-file status
of a stream is cleared by the *reset* operation.

Input buffering is normally provided on a line basis. When a program first asks for input
(using *getc*, for example) an entire line of input is read from the terminal and stored in an
internal buffer. Further input is not taken from the terminal until the existing buffered input is
read.

However, new input caused to be read by the *getbuf* operation will be buffered as a unit.
Thus, one can read in a large amount of text and allow editing of the entire amount of text. In
addition, when the internal buffer is empty, the *getc_image* operation will read a character
directly from the terminal, without interpreting it or echoing it.

The user may specify a prompt string to be printed whenever a new buffer of input is
requested from the terminal; the prompt string will also be reprinted when redisplay of the
current line is requested by the user. However, if at the time that new input is requested an
unfinished line has been output to the terminal, then that unfinished line is used instead as a
prompt.

The routine *putc_image* can be used to cause control functions, e.g. '\007' (bell) and '\p'
(new-page or clear-screen). We cannot guarantee the effect caused by any particular control
character, but we recommend that the standard ASCII interpretation of control characters be
supported wherever possible.

Terminal output may be buffered by the system up to one line at a time. However, the buffer must be flushed when new input is requested from the terminal.

Terminal streams do not have modification dates. Terminal streams should have file names and implicit line numbers.

Additional operations:

getbuf: **proctype** (stream, **string**) **returns** (**string**)
                                        signals (end_of_file, not_possible(**string**))

This operation is the same as *gets*, except that for terminals with input buffering, the new input read by *getbuf* is buffered as a unit, rather than a line at a time, allowing input editing of the entire text.

get_prompt: **proctype** (stream) **returns** (**string**)

This operation returns the current prompt string. The prompt string is initially empty (""). The empty string is returned for non-terminal streams.

set_prompt: **proctype** (stream, **string**)

This operation sets the string to be used for prompting. For non-terminal streams there is no effect.

get_input_buffered: **proctype** (stream) **returns** (**bool**)

This operation returns **true** if and only if the stream is attached to a terminal and input is being buffered.

set_input_buffered: **proctype** (stream, **bool**) **signals** (not_possible(**string**))

This operation sets the input buffering mode. Only buffered terminal input is subject to editing.

III.7. Scripting

Streams provide a mechanism for recording the input and/or output from one stream onto any number of other streams. This can be particularly useful in recording terminal sessions. The following additional operations are provided:

add_script: **proctype** (stream, stream) **signals** (script_failed)

Adds *arg2* as a script stream of *arg1*. All subsequent input from and output to *arg1* will also be output to *arg2*. Not_possible exceptions which arise in actually outputting to *arg2* will be ignored. This operation will fail if *arg2* cannot be written to, or if either stream is a direct or indirect script stream of the other.

rem_script: **proctype** (stream, stream)

Removes, but does not close, *arg2* as a (direct) script stream of *arg1*.

unscript: **proctype** (stream)

Removes, but does not close, all (direct) script streams of *arg1*.

III.8. Istreams

Istreams provide the means to read and write image files, and to perform some other operations on file objects. The operations allowed on any particular istream depend upon the access mode. In addition, certain operations may be null in some implementations.

When an operation cannot be performed, because of an incorrect access mode, because of implementation limitations, or because of properties of an individual file or device, then the operation will signal *not_possible* (unless the description of the operation explicitly says that the invocation will be ignored).

Actual reading and writing of objects is performed by *encode* and *decode* operations of the types involved. All of the built-in CLU types and type generators (except the routine type generators), and the file_name and date types, provide these operations. Designers of abstract types are encouraged to provide them also. The type specifications of the *encode* and *decode* operations for a type T are:

encode: **proctype** (T, istream) **signals** (not_possible(**string**))

For type generators, encode will have a **where** clause requiring encode operations for all components.

decode: **proctype** (istream) **returns** (T) **signals** (end_of_file, not_possible(**string**))

For type generators, decode will have a **where** clause requiring decode operations for all components.

The *encode* operations are output operations. They write an encoding of the given object onto the istream. The *decode* operations are input operations. They decode the information written by encode operations and return an object "similar" to the one encoded. If the sequence of decode operations used to read a file do not match the sequence of encode operations used to write it, then meaningless objects may be returned. The system may in some cases be able to detect this condition, in which case the decode operation will signal not_possible("bad format"). The system is not guaranteed to detect all such errors.

The istream operations are:

open: **proctype** (file_name, **string**) **returns** (istream)
                                    signals (not_possible(**string**))

The possible access modes (*arg2*) are "read", "write", and "append". If *arg2* is not one of these strings, not_possible("bad access mode") is signalled. In those cases where the system is able to detect that the specified pre-existing file is not an image file, not_possible("wrong file type") is signalled.

If the mode is "read", then the named file must exist. If the file exists, an image stream is returned upon which *decode* operations can be performed.

If the mode is "write", a new file is created or an old file is rewritten. An image stream is returned upon which *encode* operations can be performed. Write mode to storage files should guarantee exclusive access to the file, if possible.

If the mode is "append", then if the named file does not exist, one is created. An image stream is returned, positioned at the end of the file, upon which *encode* operations can be performed. Append mode to storage files should guarantee exclusive access to the file, if possible.

can_read: **proctype** (istream) **returns** (**bool**)

Can_read returns **true** if *decode* operations appear possible on the istream.

can_write: **proctype** (istream) **returns** (**bool**)

Can_write returns **true** if *encode* operations appear possible on the istream.

empty: **proctype** (istream) **returns** (**bool**)

Returns **true** if and only if there are no more objects in the file.

reset: **proctype** (istream) **signals** (not_possible(**string**))

This operation resets the istream so that the next input or output operation will read or write the first item in the file.

flush: **proctype** (istream) **signals** (not_possible(**string**))

Any buffered output is written to the file, if possible.

get_date: **proctype** (istream) **returns** (date) **signals** (not_possible(**string**))

This operation returns the date of the last modification of the corresponding storage file.

set_date: **proctype** (istream, date) **signals** (not_possible(**string**))

This operation sets the modification date of the corresponding storage file. The modification date is set automatically when a file is opened in "write" or "append" mode.

get_name: **proctype** (istream) **returns** (file_name)

This operation returns the name of the corresponding file. It may be different than the name used to open the file, in that defaults have been resolved and link indirections have been followed.

close: **proctype** (istream) **signals** (not_possible(**string**))

This operation attempts to terminate I/O and remove the association between the istream and the file. If successful, further use of operations that signal not_possible will signal not_possible. This operation will fail if buffered output cannot be written.

abort: **proctype** (istream)

This operation always terminates I/O and removes the association between the istream and the file. If buffered output cannot be written, it will be lost, and if a new file was being written, the file may or may not exist.

is_closed: **proctype** (istream) **returns (bool)**

This operation returns **true** if and only if the istream is closed.

equal: **proctype** (istream, istream) **returns (bool)**

Returns **true** if and only both arguments are the same istream.

similar: **proctype** (istream, istream) **returns (bool)**

Returns **true** if and only both arguments are the same istream.

copy: **proctype** (istream) **returns** (istream)

Returns its argument.

III.9. Miscellaneous Procedures

working_dir: **proctype () returns (string)**

This procedure returns the current working directory. The working directory is used by the I/O system to fill in a null directory in a file name.

set_working_dir: **proctype (string) signals (bad_format)**

This procedure is used to change the working directory. No checking of directory access privileges is performed.

delete_file: **proctype** (file_name) **signals** (not_possible(**string**))

This procedure deletes the specified storage file. An exception may be signalled even if the specified file does not exist, but an exception will not be signalled solely because the file does not exist. For example, an exception may be signalled if the specified directory does not exist or if the user does not have access to the directory.

rename_file: **proctype** (file_name, file_name) **signals** (not_possible(**string**))

This procedure renames the file specified by *arg1* to have the name specified by *arg2*. Renaming across directories and devices may or may not be allowed.

user_name: **proctype** () **returns** (**string**)

This procedure returns some identification of the user who is associated with the executing process.

now: **proctype** () **returns** (date)

This procedure returns the current date and time (see the next section).

e_form: **proctype** (**real, int, int**) **returns** (**string**) **signals** (illegal_field_width)

E_form returns a real literal of the form:
$$\big[-\big]i\_field\big[.f\_field\big]e\pm x\_field$$
where *i_field* is *arg2* digits, *f_field* is *arg3* digits, and *x_field* is **Exp_width** digits (see Appendix II, Section 4). If *arg3* = 0, then the decimal point and *f_field* are not present. If *arg1* ≠ 0.0, then the leftmost digit of *i_field* is not zero. If *arg1* = 0.0, then *x_field* is all zeros. Illegal_field_width occurs if *arg2* < 0 or *arg3* < 0 or *arg2* + *arg3* < 1. If necessary, *arg1* may be rounded to fit the specified form.

f_form: **proctype** (**real, int, int**) **returns** (**string**) **signals** (illegal_field_width,
insufficient_field_width)

F_form returns a real literal of the form:
$$\big[-\big]i\_field.f\_field$$
where *f_field* is *arg3* digits. If *arg2* > 0, then *i_field* is at least one digit, with leading zeros suppressed. If *arg2* = 0, then *i_field* is not present. Illegal_field_width occurs if *arg2* < 0 or *arg3* < 0 or *arg2* + *arg3* < 1. If necessary, *arg1* may be rounded to fit the specified form. Insufficient_field_width occurs if **real$exponent**(*arg1*) ≥ *arg2* after any rounding.

g_form: **proctype (real, int, int) returns (string) signals** (illegal_field_width,
                                                           insufficient_field_width)

If $arg1$ = 0.0 or $-1 \leq$ **real**\$exponent($arg1$) $< arg2$, then the result returned by this routine is f_form($arg1, arg2, arg3$).   Otherwise, the result is e_form($arg1$, 1, $arg2 + arg3$–**Exp_width**–3). Illegal_field_width occurs if $arg2 < 0$ or $arg3 < 0$ or $arg2 + arg3 < 1$. If necessary, $arg1$ may be rounded to fit the specified form.   Insufficient_field_width occurs if $arg1 \neq 0.0$ and ~($-1 \leq$ **real**\$exponent($arg1$) $< arg2$) and ($arg2 + arg3 <$ **Exp_width** + 3) after any rounding.

III.10. Dates

Dates are immutable objects that represent calendar dates and times.   The date operations are:

create: **proctype (int, int, int, int, int, int) returns (date) signals** (bad_format)

The arguments are (in order) day, month, year, hours, minutes, and seconds.

get_all: **proctype (date) returns (int, int, int, int, int, int)**

Returns the components in the same order as given to *create*.

get_day: **proctype (date) returns (int)**
get_month: **proctype (date) returns (int)**
get_year: **proctype (date) returns (int)**
get_hour: **proctype (date) returns (int)**
get_minute: **proctype (date) returns (int)**
get_second: **proctype (date) returns (int)**

(1 .. 31), (1 .. 12), (1 ..), (0 .. 23), (0 .. 59), (0 .. 59), respectively.

unparse: **proctype (date) returns (string)**

e.g., "12 January 1978 01:36:59"

unparse_date: **proctype (date) returns (string)**

e.g. "12 January 1978"

unparse_time: **proctype (date) returns (string)**

e.g. "01:36:59"

lt:	**proctype** (date, date) **returns (bool)**
le:	**proctype** (date, date) **returns (bool)**
ge:	**proctype** (date, date) **returns (bool)**
gt:	**proctype** (date, date) **returns (bool)**

The obvious relational operations; if *date1* < *date2*, then *date1* occurs earlier than *date2*.

equal: **proctype** (date, date) **returns (bool)**

The obvious equal.

similar: **proctype** (date, date) **returns (bool)**

The same as the equal operation.

copy: **proctype** (date) **returns** (date)

Copy simply returns its argument.

Appendix IV · Examples

IV.1. Priority Queue Cluster

This cluster is an implementation of priority queues. It inserts elements in $O(\log_2 n)$ time, and removes the "best" element in $O(\log_2 n)$ time, where n is the number of items in the queue, and "best" is determined by a total ordering predicate that the queue is created with.

The queue is conceptually implemented as a binary tree, balanced such that every element is "better" than its descendants, and such that the minimum depth of the tree differs from the maximum depth by at most one. The tree is actually represented by keeping the elements in an array, with the left son of $a[i]$ in $a[i \cdot 2]$, and the right son in $a[i \cdot 2 + 1]$. The root of the tree, $a[1]$, is the "best" element.

Each insertion or deletion must rebalance the tree. Since the tree is of depth strictly less than $\log_2 n$, the number of comparisons is less than $\log_2 n$ for insertion and less than $2 \log_2 n$ for removal of an element. Consequently, a sort using this technique takes less than $3 n \log_2 n$ comparisons.

This cluster illustrates the use of a type parameter, and the use of a procedure as an object.

p_queue = **cluster** [t: **type**] **is** create, best, size, empty, insert, remove

    pt = **proctype** (t, t) **returns (bool)**
    at = **array**[t]
    rep = struct[a: at, p: pt]   % 1 < i <= size(a) implies ~p(a[i], a[i/2])

% Create a p_queue with a particular sorting predicate. P should be a transitive,
% non-reflexive, total order. P(x, y) means that x is better than y. Each element in the
% p_queue should better than its sons. However, this may not be true if mutable elements are
% changed while in the p_queue.

create = **proc** (p: pt) **returns (cvt)**
        return(rep${a: at$new(), p: p})   % Low index of array must be 1 !
        end create

% Return the best element.

best = **proc** (x: **cvt**) **returns** (t) **signals** (empty)
      return(at$bottom(x.a))
        except when bounds: **signal** empty **end**
      end best

% Return the number of elements.

size = **proc** (x: **cvt**) **returns (int)**
      return(at$size(x.a))
      end size

% Return true if there are no elements.

empty = **proc** (x: **cvt**) **returns (bool)**
      return(at$empty(x.a))
      end empty

% Insert an element of type t.

```
insert = proc (x: cvt, v: t)
        a: at := x.a
        p: pt := x.p
        at$addh(a, v)                        % Make room for new item
        son: int := at$high(a)               % Tentative index of v
        dad: int := son/2                    % Get index of v's father
        while dad > 0 cand  p(v, a[dad]) do  % While v better than father
          a[son] := a[dad]                   % Move father down
          son, dad := dad, dad/2             % Get new son, father indexes
          end
        a[son] := v                          % Insert the element into place
        end insert
```

% Remove the best element and return it.

```
remove = proc (x: cvt) returns (t) signals (empty)
        a: at := x.a
        p: pt := x.p
        r: t := at$bottom(a)                 % Save best for later return
          except when bounds: signal empty end
        v: t := at$remh(a)                   % Shrink array; save element
        max_son: int := at$size(a)           % Last son node
        if max_son = 0 then return(r) end    % If now empty, we're done
        max_dad: int := max_son/2            % Last node with a son
        dad: int := 1                        % Tentative index of v
        while dad <= max_dad do              % While node has a son
          son: int := dad*2                  % Get the first son
          sval: t := a[son]
          if son < max_son                   % If there is a second son
            then nsval: t := a[son + 1]      % Find the best son
                 if p(nsval, sval) then son, sval := son + 1, nsval end
            end
          if ~p(sval, v) then break end      % If son doesn't beat v, we're done
          a[dad] := sval                     % Move son up
          dad := son                         % Move v down
          end
        a[dad] := v                          % Insert the element into place
        return(r)                            % Return the previous best element
        end remove
```

end p_queue

IV.2. Text Formatter

The following program is a simple text formatter. The input consists of a sequence of unformatted text lines mixed with command lines. Each line (except possibly the last) is terminated by a newline character, and command lines begin with a period to distinguish them from text lines. For example:

```
Justification only occurs in "fill" mode.
In "nofill" mode, each input text line is output without modification.
The .br command causes a line-break.
.br
Just like this.
```

The program produces justified, indented, and paginated text. For example:

```
Justification only occurs in "fill" mode. In "nofill"  mode,
each input text line is output without modification. The .br
command causes a line-break.
Just like this.
```

The output text is indented 10 spaces from the left margin, and is divided into pages of 50 text lines each. Each output line has 60 characters. A header of 5 lines, including a line giving the page number, is output at the beginning of each page.

An input text line consists of a sequence of words and word-break characters. The word-break characters are space, tab, and newline; all other characters are constituents of words. Tab stops are considered to be every eight spaces.

Tabs and spaces are accumulated in the current output line along with the input words. Thus, if two spaces occur in the input between two words and those words appear on the same output line, then they will be separated by at least two spaces.

The formatter has two basic modes of operation. In "nofill" mode, each input text line is output without modification. In "fill" mode, input is accepted until no more words can fit on the current output line. Newline characters are treated essentially as spaces. The line is then justified by adding extra spaces between words until the last word has its last character in the rightmost position of the line. Initially the formatter is in fill mode.

Justification is performed by enlarging spaces between words, as evenly as possible. Enlarging is performed alternately from the right and the left, starting from the right at the top of each page. Only spaces to the right of all tabs and between words are subject to justification. Furthermore, spaces preceding the first word following a tab are not subject to justification. If there are no spaces subject to justification, then no justification is performed and no error message is produced.

In fill mode, any input line that starts with a word-break character causes a line-break: the current output line is neither filled nor adjusted, but is output as is. An "empty" input line (one starting with a newline character) causes a line-break and then causes a blank line to be output.

In nofill mode, if an input line is longer than the line length, it is output as given with no error message. In fill mode, if a word is longer than the line length, it is output as given on a line by itself with no error message.

The formatter accepts three different commands:

> .br - causes a line-break
> .nf - causes a line-break, and changes the mode to "nofill"
> .fi - causes a line-break, and changes the mode to "fill"

An unrecognized command name causes an error message and is otherwise ignored.

The program performs input and output on streams.

Fig. 8. Module Dependency Diagram

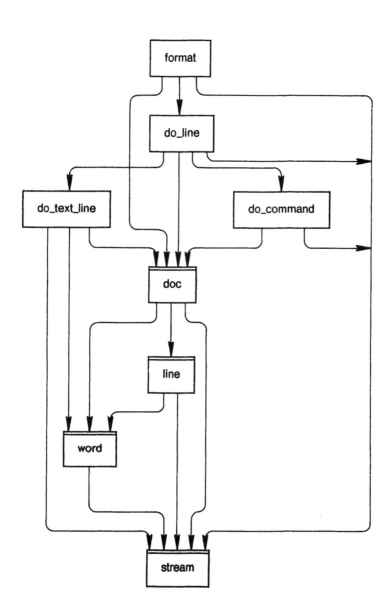

Note: boxes with a double line at the top indicate clusters.

% Read the instream, processing it and placing the output on outstream and writing error
% messages on errstream.

```
format = proc (instream, outstream, errstream: stream) signals (bad_arg(string))
          if ~stream$can_read(instream) then signal bad_arg("input stream")
            elseif ~stream$can_write(outstream) then signal bad_arg("output stream")
            elseif ~stream$can_write(errstream) then signal bad_arg("error stream")
            end
          d: doc := doc$create(outstream)
          while ~stream$empty(instream) do
            line: int := instream.lineno
            do_line(instream, d)
              except when error (why: string):
                            stream$putl(errstream, int$unparse(line) || ":\t" || why)
                      end
            end
          doc$terminate(d)
          end format
```

% Process an input line. The line is processed either as a text line or as a command line,
% depending upon whether or not the first character of the line is a period.

```
do_line = proc (instream: stream, d: doc) signals (error(string))
          c: char := stream$peekc(instream)
          if c = '.'
            then do_command(instream, d)
                    resignal error
            else do_text_line(instream, d)
            end
          end do_line
```

% Process a command line. This procedure reads up to the first space or tab in a line and
% processes the string read as a command. The remainder of the line is read and discarded.

```
do_command = proc (instream: stream, d: doc) signals (error(string))
            stream$getc(instream)       % skip the period
            n: string := stream$gets(instream, " \t\n")
              except when end_of_file: n := "" end
            stream$getl(instream)       % read and discard remainder of input line
              except when end_of_file: end
            if n = "br" then doc$break_line(d)
              elseif n = "fi" then doc$set_fill(d)
              elseif n = "nf" then doc$set_nofill(d)
              elseif n = "" then signal error("missing command")
              else signal error("'" || n || "' not a command")
              end
            end do_command
```

% Process a text line. This procedure reads one line from instream and processes it as a text
% line. If the first character is a word-break character, then a line-break is caused. If the line
% is empty, then a blank line is output. Otherwise, the words and word-break characters in
% the line are processed in turn.

```
do_text_line = proc (instream: stream, d: doc)
               c: char := stream$getc(instream)
               if c = '\n'
                 then doc$skip_line(d)       % empty input line
                         return
                elseif c = ' ' cor c = '\t'
                 then doc$break_line(d)
                end
                while c ~= '\n' do
                  if c = ' ' then doc$add_space(d)
                    elseif c = '\t' then doc$add_tab(d)
                    else w: word := word$scan(c, instream)
                         doc$add_word(d, w)
                    end
                  c := stream$getc(instream)
                  end except when end_of_file: end
               doc$add_newline(d)
               end do_text_line
```

% The doc cluster implements documents, the properly indented, justified, and paginated
% output of the text formatter. A document is constructed incrementally, using operations to
% add words, spaces, tabs, and newlines to the end of the document. Other operations are
% used for the basic formatting actions: break_line to cause a line break, skip_line to output a
% blank line, set_fill and set_nofill to set the formatting mode. Rather than collecting the
% entire document as a sequence of lines before outputting to a file, each line is output as it
% is produced. The current output line is maintained for the purposes of performing
% justification. To perform pagination and the production of headings, the current line
% number and the current page number are also maintained.

```
doc = cluster is create, add_word, add_space, add_tab, add_newline,
                break_line, skip_line, set_fill, set_nofill, terminate


    rep = record[line:      line,    % The current line.
                 fill:      bool,    % True iff in fill mode.
                 r2l:       bool,    % True iff justify next line right-to-left.
                 lineno:    int,     % The number of lines output so far on this page
                                     % (not including any header lines).
                 pageno:    int,     % The number of the current output page.
                 outstream: stream]  % The output stream.

    chars_per_line = 60
    lines_per_page = 50
    left_margin_size = 10
```

% Create a doc object. The first page is number 1, there are no lines yet output on it. Fill
% mode is in effect.

```
create = proc (outstream: stream) returns (cvt)
        return(rep${line:      line$create(),
                    fill:      true,
                    r2l:       true,
                    lineno:    0,
                    pageno:    1,
                    outstream: outstream})
        end create
```

% Process a word. This procedure adds the word W to the output document. If in nofill
% mode, then the word is simply added to the end of the current line (there is no line-length
% checking in nofill mode). If in fill mode, then we first check to see if there is room for the
% word on the current line. If the word will not fit on the current line, we first justify and
% output the line and then start a new one; justification is performed alternately from the right
% and the left on successive lines. However, if the line is empty, then we just add the word to
% the end of the line; if the word won't fit on an empty line, then it won't fit on any line, so we
% have no choice but to put it on the current line, even if it doesn't fit.

```
add_word = proc (d: cvt, w: word)
             if d.fill cand ~line$empty(d.line)
               then if line$length(d.line) + word$width(w) > chars_per_line
                      then line$justify(d.line, chars_per_line, d.r2l)
                           d.r2l := ~d.r2l
                           output_line(d)
                    end
             end
             line$add_word(d.line, w)
             end add_word
```

% Process a space -- just add it to the current line.

```
add_space = proc (d: cvt)
             line$add_space(d.line)
             end add_space
```

% Process a tab -- just add it to the current line.

```
add_tab = proc (d: cvt)
             line$add_tab(d.line)
             end add_tab
```

% Process a newline. If in nofill mode, then the current line is output as is. Otherwise, a
% newline is treated just like a space.

```
add_newline = proc (d: cvt)
             if ~d.fill
               then output_line(d)
               else line$add_space(d.line)
               end
             end add_newline
```

% Cause a line break. If the line is not empty, then it is output as is. Line breaks have no
% effect on empty lines -- multiple line breaks are the same as one.

```
break_line = proc (d: cvt)
                  if ~line$empty(d.line) then output_line(d) end
                  end break_line
```

% Cause a line break and output a blank line.

```
skip_line = proc (d: cvt)
              break_line(up(d))
              output_line(d)        % line is empty
              end skip_line
```

% Cause a line break and enter fill mode.

```
set_fill = proc (d: cvt)
             break_line(up(d))
             d.fill := true
             end set_fill
```

% Cause a line break and enter nofill mode.

```
set_nofill = proc (d: cvt)
               break_line(up(d))
               d.fill := false
               end set_nofill
```

% Terminate the output document.

```
terminate = proc (d: cvt)
              break_line(up(d))
              end terminate
```

% Internal routine.

% Output line is used to keep track of the line number and the page number and to put out
% the header at the top of each page. At the top of each page, justification is reset to start
% from the right.

```
output_line = proc (d: rep)
            if d.lineno = 0
              then if d.pageno > 1
                      then stream$putc(d.outstream, '\p') end
                    stream$puts(d.outstream, "\n\n")      % print header
                    stream$putspace(d.outstream, left_margin_size)
                    stream$puts(d.outstream, "Page ")
                    stream$puts(d.outstream, int$unparse(d.pageno))
                    stream$puts(d.outstream, "\n\n\n")
                end
            d.lineno := d.lineno + 1
            if ~line$empty(d.line)
              then stream$putspace(d.outstream, left_margin_size)
                    line$output(d.line, d.outstream)
                end
            stream$putc(d.outstream, '\n')
            if d.lineno = lines_per_page
              then d.r2l := true
                    d.lineno := 0
                    d.pageno := d.pageno + 1
                end
            end output_line

end doc
```

% A line is a mutable sequence of words, spaces, and tabs. The length of a line is the number
% of character positions that would be used if the line were output. One may output a line
% onto a stream, in which case the line is made empty after printing. One may also justify a
% line to a given length, which means that some spaces in the line will be enlarged to make
% the length of the line equal to the desired length. Only spaces to the right of all tabs are
% subject to justification. Furthermore, spaces preceding the first word in the output line or
% preceding the first word following a tab are not subject to justification. If there are no
% spaces subject to justification or if the line is too long, then no justification is performed
% and no error message is produced.

line = **cluster is** create, add_word, add_space, add_tab, length, empty, justify, output

```
        token = variant[space: int,       % the int is the width of the space
                          tab:   int,       % the int is the width of the tab
                        word:  word]
        at = array[token]
        rep = record[length: int,          % the current length of the line
                     stuff:   at]          % the contents of the line
                                            % no two adjacent tokens will both be spaces

        max_tab_width = 8                  % maximum chars per tab
```

% Create an empty line.

```
create = proc () returns (cvt)
        return(rep${length: 0,
                    stuff:    at$new()})
        end create
```

% Add a word at the end of the line.

```
add_word = proc (l: cvt, w: word)
              at$addh(l.stuff, token$make_word(w))
              l.length := l.length + word$width(w)
              end add_word
```

% Add a space at the end of the line, combining it with an existing trailing space, if any.

```
add_space = proc (l: cvt)
              l.length := l.length + 1
              tagcase at$top(l.stuff)
                tag space (width: int): token$change_space(at$top(l.stuff), width + 1)
                                        return
                others:
                end except when bounds: end   % Handle empty array case.
              at$addh(l.stuff, token$make_space(1))
              end add_space
```

% Add a tab at the end of the line.

```
add_tab = proc (l: cvt)
            width: int := max_tab_width – (l.length // max_tab_width)
            l.length := l.length + width
            at$addh(l.stuff, token$make_tab(width))
            end add_tab
```

% Return the current length of the line.

```
length = proc (l: cvt) returns (int)
            return(l.length)
            end length
```

% Return true if the line is of length zero.

```
empty = proc (l: cvt) returns (bool)
            return(l.length = 0)
            end empty
```

% Justify the line, if possible, so that it's length is equal to LEN. Before justification, any
% trailing space is removed. If the line length at that point is greater or equal to the desired
% length, then no action is taken. Otherwise, the set of justifiable spaces is found, as
% described above. If there are no justifiable spaces, then no further action is taken.
% Otherwise, the justifiable spaces are enlarged, as evenly as possible, to make the line
% length the desired length.   Enlarging is performed either from the right or the left,
% depending on R2L.

```
justify = proc (l: cvt, len: int, r2l: bool)
            tagcase at$top(l.stuff)
              tag space (width: int): at$remh(l.stuff)
                                      l.length := l.length – width
              others:
              end except when bounds: end % Handle empty array case.
            if l.length >= len then return end
            diff: int := len – l.length
            first: int := find_first_justifiable_space(l)
              except when none: return end
            enlarge_spaces(l, first, diff, r2l)
            end justify
```

% Output the line and reset it.

```
output = proc (l: cvt, outstream: stream)
        for t: token in at$elements(l.stuff) do
          tagcase t
            tag word (w: word): word$output(w, outstream)
            tag space, tab (width: int): stream$putspace(outstream, width)
            end
          end
        l.length := 0
        at$trim(l.stuff, 1, 0)
        end output
```

% Internal routines.

% Find the first justifiable space. This space is the first space after the first word after the last
% tab in the line. Return the index of the space in the array. Signal NONE if there are no
% justifiable spaces. Although no two adjacent tokens will both be words (as lines are
% currently used), no such assumption is made here.

```
find_first_justifiable_space = proc (l: rep) returns (int) signals (none)
        a: at := l.stuff
        if at$empty(a) then signal none end
        lo: int := at$low(a)
        hi: int := at$high(a)
        i: int := hi
        while i > lo cand ~token$is_tab(a[i]) do      % find last tab in the line (if any)
          i := i - 1
          end
        while i <= hi cand ~token$is_word(a[i]) do % find first word after it
          i := i + 1
          end
        while i <= hi cand ~token$is_space(a[i]) do% find first space after that
          i := i + 1
          end
        if i > hi then signal none end
        return(i)
        end find_first_justifiable_space
```

```
% Enlarge the spaces in the array whose indexes are at least FIRST.  Add a total of DIFF extra
% character widths of space.  Add spaces working from the right or the left, depending on
% R2L.

enlarge_spaces = proc (l: rep, first, diff: int, r2l: bool)
                  nspaces, last: int := count_spaces(l, first)
                  if nspaces = 0 then return end
                  by: int := 1
                  if r2l
                    then by := -1
                         first, last := last, first
                    end
                  neach: int := diff / nspaces        % Amount to increase each space.
                  nextra: int := diff // nspaces      % Leftovers to be distributed.
                  for i: int in int$from_to_by(first, last, by) do
                    tagcase l.stuff[i]
                       tag space (width: int): width := width + neach
                                              if nextra > 0
                                                then width := width + 1
                                                     nextra := nextra - 1
                                                end
                                              token$change_space(l.stuff[i], width)
                       others:
                       end
                    end
                  l.length := l.length + diff
                  end enlarge_spaces

% Return a count of the number of spaces in the line whose indexes in the array are at least
% IDX, and return the index of the last space counted.

count_spaces = proc (l: rep, idx: int) returns (int, int)
                  count: int := 0
                  for i: int in int$from_to(idx, at$high(l.stuff)) do
                    tagcase l.stuff[i]
                       tag space: count := count + 1
                                  idx := i
                       others:
                       end
                    end
                  return(count, idx)
                  end count_spaces

end line
```

% A word is an item of text. It may be output to a stream. It has a width, which is the number
% of character positions that are taken up when the word is printed.

word = **cluster is** scan, width, output

    rep = **string**

% Construct a word whose first character is C and whose remaining characters are to be
% removed from the instream.

```
scan = proc (c: char, instream: stream) returns (cvt)
        s: string := string$c2s(c)
        s := s || stream$gets(instream, " \t\n")
          except when end_of_file: end
        return(s)
        end scan
```

% Return the width of the word.

```
width = proc (w: cvt) returns (int)
        return(string$size(w))
        end width
```

% Output the word.

```
output = proc (w: cvt, outstream: stream)
        stream$puts(outstream, w)
        end output
```

```
end word
```

IV.3. Text Substitution Program

The following (rather complex) program performs textual substitutions of one set of strings for another throughout a file. It can be useful in expanding abbreviations, renaming variables, correcting misspellings, etc.

Substitutions are specified by a list of rules read from a file. Each rule consists of a left-hand-side (the string to be replaced) and a right-hand-side (the string to replace with), separated by a '>' character. Each rule is terminated by a newline character. For example, to substitute "BEGIN" for "begin" and "END" for "end", the rules would be:

```
begin>BEGIN
end>END
```

All substitutions are done simultaneously, so for example it is possible to substitute "a" for "b" and "b" for "a". Substitution is not performed on the results of a substitution, only on the original text. When performing substitutions, the rule with the longest left-hand-side always takes precedence. Thus, given the two rules:

```
abc>x
a>y
```

an input of "abcab" would be transformed to "xyb".

Within a rule, characters can be represented with the same escape sequences allowed in string literals. For example, the following rule replaces each newline by two newlines:

```
\n>\n\n
```

In addition, the escape sequence "\>" can be used to represent the character ">".

The program asks for the name of a rule file, and then loops asking for pairs of input and output file names to process using the given rules. If no input file is given, a new rule file is requested. If no rule file is given, the program terminates. If no output file is given, a new input file is requested.

The program is implemented using a pushdown transducer: a pushdown automaton extended to produce output.

Fig. 9. Module Dependency Diagram

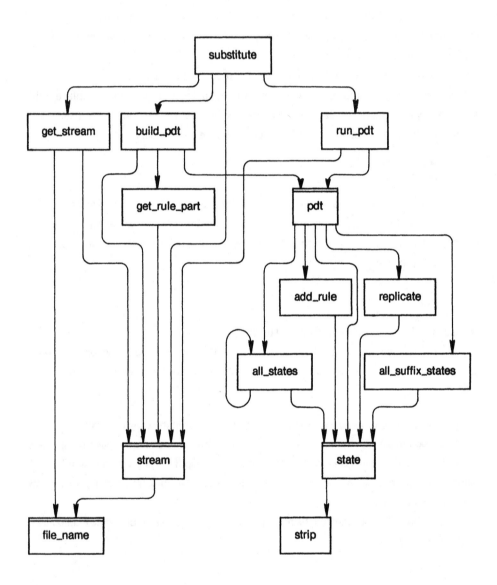

Note: boxes with a double line at the top indicate clusters.

% Ask for a rule file and build a pushdown transducer for it, and then loop asking for pairs of
% input and output files and processing them using that pushdown transducer. When no
% input file is given, ask for a new rule file. When no rule file is given, terminate. When no
% output file is given, ask for a new input file.

```
substitute = proc ()
            tyo: stream := stream$primary_output()
            while true do
              rst: stream := get_stream("rule file: ", "read")
                except when refused: return end
              m: pdt := build_pdt(rst)
                except when illegal (line: int, why: string):
                            stream$close(rst)
                            stream$putl(tyo, int$unparse(line) || ":\t" || why)
                            continue
                      end
              stream$close(rst)
              while true do
                inst: stream := get_stream("input file: ", "read")
                  except when refused: break end
                outst: stream := get_stream("output file: ", "write")
                  except when refused: stream$close(inst)
                                    continue
                        end
                run_pdt(inst, outst, m)
                stream$close(outst)
                stream$close(inst)
                end
              end
            end substitute
```

% Read in a file_name and open the file in the given mode. Signal refused if no file_name is
% given.

```
get_stream = proc (prompt, mode: string) returns (stream) signals (refused)
              tyi: stream := stream$primary_input()
              tyo: stream := stream$primary_output()
              tyi.input_buffered := true
              while true do
                stream$puts(tyo, prompt)
                fs: string := stream$getl(tyi)
                if string$empty(fs)
                  then signal refused end
                return(stream$open(file_name$parse(fs), mode))
                  except when bad_format: stream$putl(tyo, "bad format file name")
                         when not_possible (s: string): stream$putl(tyo, s)
                         end
                end except when end_of_file: signal refused end
              end get_stream
```

% Read and parse the rules from the given stream. Construct and return a pushdown
% transducer corresponding to those rules.

```
build_pdt = proc (st: stream) returns (pdt) signals (illegal(int, string))
             rule = struct[left, right: string]
             rulelist = array[rule]
             rules: rulelist := rulelist$new()
             while true do
               while stream$peekc(st) = '\n' do
                 stream$getc(st)
                 end except when end_of_file: return(pdt$create(rules)) end
               left: string := get_rule_part(st, ">\n")
               if string$empty(left)
                 then signal illegal(st.lineno, "missing left side of rule") end
               if stream$empty(st) cor stream$getc(st) ~= '>'
                 then signal illegal(st.lineno, "missing right side of rule") end
               right: string := get_rule_part(st, "\n")
               rulelist$addh(rules, rule${left: left, right: right})
               end except when illegal (why: string): signal illegal(st.lineno, why) end
             end build_pdt
```

% Parses a rule part up to but not including the given terminators. Accepts the regular
% escape sequences, plus "\>" to represent ">".

```
get_rule_part = proc (st: stream, terms: string) returns (string) signals (illegal(string))
                terms := string$append(terms, '\\')
                part: string := ""
                while true do
                  begin
                  part := part || stream$gets(st, terms)
                  if stream$peekc(st) ~= '\\'
                    then return(part) end
                  end except when end_of_file: return(part) end
                  c: char := stream$getc(st)
                  x: int := string$indexc(stream$peekc(st), "'\"\\>ntpbrv")
                  if x > 0
                    then stream$getc(st)
                         c := "'\"\\>\n\t\p\b\r\v"[x]
                    else sum: int := 0
                         for i: int in int$from_to(1, 3) do
                           c := stream$getc(st)
                           if c < '0' cor c > '7'
                             then exit illegal_char end
                           sum := sum * 8 + char$c2i(c) - char$c2i('0')
                           end
                         c := char$i2c(sum)
                    end
                  part := string$append(part, c)
                  end
                except when end_of_file, illegal_char:
                              signal illegal("bad escape sequence")
                        end
                end get_rule_part
```

% Perform all substitutions on a file.

```
run_pdt = proc (inst, outst: stream, m: pdt)
          while true do
            pdt$move(m, stream$getc(inst))
              except when output (s: string): stream$puts(outst, s) end
            end except when end_of_file: stream$puts(outst, pdt$reset(m)) end
          end run_pdt
```

% A pushdown transducer is a collection of states connected by transitions. A transition can
% also connect a state to an output condition, with the initial state as the implicit next state. A
% transition is labeled with both an input character and a set of lookahead characters; the
% transition is to be followed if the current input character matches and the current
% lookahead character is in the lookahead set. The basic operation of the transducer is
% move, which moves according to the current input character (at the top of the pushdown
% list), and the current lookahead character (given as an argument). Output is produced by
% signalling with a string result.

```
pdt = cluster is create, move, reset

    rep = record[first:     state,      % initial state
                 buffer:    buf,        % path from initial state to current state
                                        % plus next input char
                 current:   state]      % current state

    rule = struct[left, right: string]
    rulelist = array[rule]
    buf = array[char]
```

% Two phase construction. First construct all states and transitions needed to follow any
% single rule from the initial state to its output condition. Then fill in missing cross-transitions
% for rules that interact with each other, in (approximately) the following manner. For each
% substring of a left-hand side of a rule (a path from some state S3 to some state S2) that is
% also a prefix of a left-hand side of a rule (a path from the initial state to some state S1), add
% all transitions out of S1 (not conflicting with existing transitions out of S2) as transitions out
% of S2.

```
create = proc (rules: rulelist) returns (cvt) signals (illegal(string))
          first: state := state$create()
          for r: rule in rulelist$elements(rules) do
            add_rule(first, r)
            end resignal illegal
          for path: string, s2: state in all_states(first) do
            for s1: state in all_suffix_states(path, first) do
              replicate(s1, s2)
              end
            end
          return(rep${first: first,  buffer: buf$new(),  current: first})
          end create
```

% Make a move with the given char as the lookahead input. If a rule is recognized (an output
% condition is reached), the left side of the rule is discarded from the end of the buffered
% input, and any remaining input is concatenated with the right side of the rule and returned
% for output. If no rule can match the current buffered input, the entire buffered input is
% returned for output.

```
move = proc (m: cvt, peek: char) signals (output(string))
        m.current := state$move(m.current, buf$top(m.buffer), peek)
          except when output (size: int, out: string):
                        buf$trim(m.buffer, 1, buf$size(m.buffer) – size)
                        out := reset1(m) || out
                        buf$addh(m.buffer, peek)
                        signal output(out)
              when no_match:
                        out: string := reset1(m)
                        buf$addh(m.buffer, peek)
                        signal output(out)
              when bounds:
              end
        buf$addh(m.buffer, peek)
        end move
```

% Force input termination. Returns any final output. Restores the pdt to its initial state.

```
reset = proc (m: cvt) returns (string)
        extra: string := ""
        m.current := state$move1(m.current, buf$top(m.buffer))
          except when output (size: int, out: string):
                        buf$trim(m.buffer, 1, buf$size(m.buffer) – size)
                        extra := out
              when no_match, bounds:
              end
        return(reset1(m) || extra)
        end reset
```

% Internal routine.

% Return current buffered input. Reset current state to initial state.

```
reset1 = proc (m: rep) returns (string)
        s: string := string$ac2s(m.buffer)
        buf$trim(m.buffer, 1, 0)
        m.current := m.first
        return(s)
        end reset1
```

end pdt

% Add a new rule. Follow existing path through pdt as far as possible, and then add new
% states. Just add states and transitions needed to follow the rule from the initial state to the
% output condition, do not add cross-transitions for interacting rules.

```
add_rule = proc (s: state, r: rule) signals (illegal(string))
            rule = struct[left, right: string]
            left: string := r.left
            if string$empty(left)
              then signal illegal("rule has empty left side") end
            size: int := string$size(left)
            i: int := 1
            peeks: string := ""
            while i < size do
              s := state$move(s, left[i], left[i + 1])
              i := i + 1
              end except when output (•): peeks := string$c2s(left[i + 1])
                         when no_match:
                         end
            while i < size do
              ns: state := state$create()
              state$add_move(s, left[i], peeks, ns)
              s := ns
              i := i + 1
              peeks := ""
              end
            state$add_output(s, left[size], size, r.right)
              except when illegal: signal illegal("conflicting rules") end
            end add_rule
```

% Traverse depth first left to right, yielding all path-state pairs reachable from given state.
% Depth first traversal is used to satisfy the requirement that the rule with the longest
% left-hand side takes precedence.

```
all_states = iter (s: state) yields (string, state)
            for input: char, peeks: string, next: state in state$all_moves(s) do
              pre: string := string$c2s(input)
              for path: string, ns: state in all_states(next) do
                yield(pre || path, ns)
                end
              yield(pre, next)
              end
            end all_states
```

% Given a string, follow all proper suffixes (longest first) of the string as paths from the given
% state, and yield the final state reached by each legal path. The suffixes are done longest
% first to satisfy the requirement that the rule with the longest left-hand side takes
% precedence.

```
all_suffix_states = iter (path: string, first: state) yields (state)
                   size: int := string$size(path)
                   for i: int in int$from_to(2, size) do
                     s: state := first
                     j: int := i
                     while j < size do
                       s := state$move(s, path[j], path[j + 1])
                       j := j + 1
                       end except others: continue end
                     s := state$move1(s, path[j])
                       except others: continue end
                     yield(s)
                     end
                   end all_suffix_states
```

% For each input char causing a transition out of S1 but not causing a transition out of S2,
% add a transition out of S2.

```
replicate = proc (s1, s2: state)
            for input: char, peeks: string, s: state in state$all_moves(s1) do
              state$move1(s2, input)
                except when output (*): continue
                       when no_match:
                       end
              state$add_move(s2, input, peeks, s)
                except others: end
              end
            for input: char, size: int, out: string in state$all_outputs(s1) do
              state$add_output(s2, input, size, out)
                except others: end
              end
            end replicate
```

% A state is a collection of arcs, each labeled with the input character required to take the
% transition. An arc either points to a new state, or indicates an output condition (with the
% initial state as the implicit new state). For arcs to new states, a list of acceptable lookahead
% characters is also present, with an empty list indicating "all others". An output condition
% implicitly carries an "all others" lookahead list.   There are operations to add new
% transitions, iterate over the transitions, and move to a new state given the current input and
% lookahead.

state = **cluster is** create, all_moves, add_move, all_outputs, add_output, move, move1

```
rep = array[trans]                  % a state is a set of transitions
trans = struct[input: char,         % a transition is a labeled arc
              next: arc]
arc = oneof[state:  pstate,         % an arc is to a new state
            output: output]         % or to an output condition
pstate = record[peeks: string,      % empty lookahead means "all others"
               state:  state]
output = struct[size: int,          % size of left side of rule
               out: string]         % right side of rule
                                    % implicit "all others" lookahead
```

% Create a new state with no transitions.

```
create = proc () returns (cvt)
        return(rep$new())
        end create
```

% Yield all transitions (input, lookaheads, next state) from the given state to new states.

```
all_moves = iter (s: cvt) yields (char, string, state)
            for t: trans in rep$elements(s) do
              tagcase t.next
              tag state (ps: pstate): yield(t.input, ps.peeks, ps.state)
              tag output:
              end
            end
          end all_moves
```

% Add a transition from one state to another for the given input and that subset of the given
% list of lookahead chars not present on existing transitions for the given input. The addition
% is illegal if all of the lookaheads are already accounted for by existing transitions. An
% empty lookahead list denotes "all others not specified on other transitions for the same
% input".

```
add_move = proc (from: cvt, input: char, peeks: string, to: state) signals (illegal)
           rpeeks: string := peeks
           for t: trans in rep$elements(from) do
             if t.input = input
               then tagcase t.next
                       tag state (ps: pstate): if string$empty(ps.peeks)
                                                 then signal illegal
                                                 else rpeeks := strip(rpeeks, ps.peeks)
                                                 end
                       tag output: if string$empty(peeks)
                                     then signal illegal end
                   end
             end
           end
           if string$empty(rpeeks) cand ~string$empty(peeks)
             then signal illegal end
           rep$addl(from, trans${input: input,
                             next: arc$make_state(pstate${peeks: peeks,
                                                          state: to})})
           end add_move
```

% Yield all transitions (input, size, output) from the given state to output conditions.

```
all_outputs = iter (s: cvt) yields (char, int, string)
           for t: trans in rep$elements(s) do
             tagcase t.next
               tag state:
               tag output (x: output): yield(t.input, x.size, x.out)
               end
             end
           end all_outputs
```

% Add a transition from the given state to an output condition for the given input. An "all
% others" lookahead list is implicit for this transition, so the addition is illegal if a transition for
% the given input and an "all others" lookahead list already exists.

```
add_output = proc (from: cvt, input: char, size: int, out: string) signals (illegal)
            for t: trans in rep$elements(from) do
                if t.input = input
                  then tagcase t.next
                          tag state (ps: pstate):
                                if ~string$empty(ps.peeks)
                                  then continue end
                                peeks: string := ""
                                for x: trans in rep$elements(down(ps.state)) do
                                  peeks := string$append(peeks, x.input)
                                  end
                                ps.peeks := peeks
                          tag output:
                                signal illegal
                          end
                  end
              end
            rep$addh(from, trans${input: input,
                            next: arc$make_output(output${size: size,
                                                          out: out})})
            end add_output
```

% Return the next state for the given input and lookahead. Signal no_match if no transition is
% possible. Signal output if an output condition is reached.

```
move = proc (s: cvt, input, peek: char) returns (state)
                                    signals (no_match, output(int, string))
        for t: trans in rep$elements(s) do
          if t.input = input
            then tagcase t.next
                    tag state (ps: pstate):
                          if string$empty(ps.peeks) cor string$indexc(peek, ps.peeks) > 0
                            then return(ps.state) end
                    tag output (x: output):
                          signal output(x.size, x.out)
                    end
            end
          end
        signal no_match
        end move
```

% Return the next state for the given input with no further input available. Signal no_match if
% no transition is possible. Signal output if an output condition is reached.

```
move1 = proc (s: cvt, input: char) returns (state) signals (no_match, output(int, string))
        for t: trans in rep$elements(s) do
          if t.input = input
            then tagcase t.next
                    tag state (ps: pstate): if string$empty(ps.peeks)
                                              then return(ps.state) end
                    tag output (x: output): signal output(x.size, x.out)
                    end
            end
          end
        signal no_match
        end move1

end state
```

% Remove chars in USING from chars in FROM.

```
strip = proc (from, using: string) returns (string)
        for c: char in string$chars(using) do
          i: int := string$indexc(c, from)
          if i > 0
            then from := string$substr(from, 1, i – 1) || string$rest(from, i + 1) end
          end
        return(from)
        end strip
```

Index

Operators and Punctuation